W9-AAM-598

THE SECOND COMING

of the WOOLLY MAMMOTH

An Entrepreneur's Bible

TED FROST

TEN SPEED PRESS
BERKELEY, CALIFORNIA

Copyright © 1991 by Ted S. Frost. All rights reserved. No part of this book may be reproduced in any form, except for brief reviews, without the written permission of the publisher.

TEN SPEED PRESS
P.O. Box 7123
Berkeley, California 94707

Permission to use the following copyrighted material is gratefully acknowledged: "Belvedere" by M. C. Escher. © 1991 M. C. Escher Heirs/Cordon Art, Baarn, Holland. "Protect Our Wild Life" by Don Martin. © 1974 E. C. Publications. From "Heavy Stomachs" by Edmond York. © 1958 by Edmond York. "Out of Court Settlement" by Charles Bragg. © 1981 by Charles Bragg. "Accountant Street Gangs" by Gary Larson. © 1987 by Universal Press Syndicate. Reprinted with permission. All rights reserved. "In the Animal Self-Help Section," and "Never Look Back, Something Might Be Gaining On You" by Gary Larson. © 1980, 1984 by Chronicle Features. THE FAR SIDE cartoons by Gary Larson are reprinted by permission of Chronicle Features, San Francisco, CA.

Cover design by Nancy Austin
Cover illustration by Ellen Sasaki
Text design and typography by Wilsted & Taylor

LIBRARY OF CONGRESS CATALOGING-IN-PUBLICATION DATA

Frost, Ted S., 1932–
    The second coming of the woolly mammoth : an entrepreneur's bible / Ted S. Frost.
      p. cm.
    ISBN 0-89815-407-3
    1. Small business—Management.   2. New business enterprises.   3. Entrepreneurship.   I. Title.
HD69.S6F76   1991
658.02'2—dc20   90-19219
                                     CIP

Printed in the United States of America

1 2 3 4 5 – 95 94 93 92 91

*To the small business people and
entrepreneurs of America, whose energy and
enterprise helped capitalism win the Cold War
without a shot being fired.*

CONTENTS

INTRODUCTION

Once upon a time many tax returns ago, I wrote a book called *Where Have All the Woolly Mammoths Gone?: A Small Business Survival Manual.* *Woolly Mammoths* was favorably received. As a matter of fact, it turned into something of a cult book among small business owners. I still hear from people wanting a copy. To the point, a sequel-update seems in order. So here it is: *The Second Coming of the Woolly Mammoth.*

The original book was a distillation of my experiences as a CPA spending most of his career with small business clients. It was written from the point of view that small business is slowly dying out in this country and is on its way to extinction, *à la* the woolly mammoth. That, after all, is what 90 years of government statistics showed at the time.

Guess what? After *Woolly Mammoth*'s publication, the slow death trend of small business reversed itself. Because of far-reaching changes in the economy, opportunities have exploded for entrepreneurs. Start-up companies are now being created at a record rate. Small business constitutes the biggest source of new jobs today and is an important contributor to gross national product. Much, I might add, to my surprise. And very much a pleasant surprise, too, for I am an unabashed fan of small business. I believe everyone should try being self-employed at least once in their lives. Even if you should fail (which in terms of probabilities is more likely than not), the experience of being your own boss will make you a wiser person and a more informed citizen. I guarantee it.

So this rendition of *Woolly Mammoths* is optimistic in recognition of the improved environment for small business and the joys of personal growth connected with owning your own business. The original book's ideas have been updated and a substantial amount of new material has been added. These changes reflect my being pummeled by more years of experience as well as the fact that this old world has seen some dramatic developments in the interim.

I have a big advantage over other small business authors. Most people writing on the subject are limited to their own personal experiences. In contrast, I have the experiences of thousands of small business clients to draw upon as well as my own. In addition, most authors portray themselves as successful superstars with the pitch, "Follow my advice and you too can be fabulously successful." Well, I'm no superstar. I've made about every mistake there is. And those I've missed, my clients have made. My message is: Avoid our mistakes and you probably will survive, you may prosper, and, if lightning strikes, you might just hit the jackpot.

This is an easy book to read but a difficult one to assimilate. It covers a large range of topics and hops from generalities to specifics and back to generalities again. But that is life itself. Wisdom is a process of slow accretion rather than silver bullet revelations. I hope, then, that the words that follow will help guide you through entrepreneurship's perilous but exciting waters.

PART ONE

BACKGROUND CONSIDERATIONS

CHAPTER 1

LEARN FROM

THE EXPERIENCES OF OTHERS

History repeats itself. That's one of the things wrong with history.   Clarence Darrow

Given my background, the fact that I became a CPA is ironic. What's doubly ironic is that I became successful as one. Let's face it, I'm a lousy accountant. For over 30 years I've made a good living as a CPA, but now it's confession time. The truth is, I can't stand details, columns of figures bore me, and sorting numbers drives me up the wall. I'd rather break rocks with a sledge than crunch numbers with a pencil. So, what's my excuse for writing as a CPA on small business? You are entitled to an answer before wading into this book much further.

I've got good reasons for pontificating on small business, because I'm not writing as a CPA. I'm writing as a voyeur, a "Peeping Tom" observer of thousands of small business ventures. Peeking through the keyholes of my CPA practice, I've witnessed the whole spectrum. From small business successes to small business muddlings along to small business failures.

So what? So have many other long-time CPAs. Ah, but the difference is, I've been interested in the people involved rather than the numbers created. I could care less about balancing their books. It's the human stories that interested me.

How did I end up as an accountant if I'm not interested in the number side of things? I didn't start out wanting to be a CPA, that's for sure. My original career goal, believe it or not, was zoology. Biology and science courses were what turned me on as a young man. By the time I was a junior in college, though, it had become apparent that zoology is a hardscrabble way to make a living. You don't find many help wanted ads for zoologists listed in the classified ad sections of newspapers.

Recognizing the gap between my wants and my resources, I belatedly transferred into the school of business administration. Now, you can't just major in business. You must have a specific major within that general field. As I perused the business school curriculum, accounting, beginning with *a*, caught my eye. I knew nothing about the subject but assumed it had something to do with counting money. And I remembered what the famous bank robber, Willie Sutton, once said. When asked why he robbed banks, Willie replied, "Because that's where the money is."

Willie Sutton makes sense. If you are setting out to make money, it only stands to reason you should first try to find out where the money is located. It looked to me as if accounting would be a good place to start.

Little did I realize back then that walking away from the profession of zoology would lead me right into the middle of a zoo—the business world zoo. As a matter of fact, it's more than a zoo. The business world is a jungle out there! In it, you will find all sorts of creatures: turkeys, sharks, jackasses, old goats, dingbats, bearcats, tigers, pussy cats, dodoes, leeches, old-dogs-that-can't-be-taught-new-tricks, ratfinks, snakes-in-the-grass, louses, crazy-like-foxes, parasites . . . the menagerie goes on and on. So, for someone like myself interested in studying animal life, accounting turned out to be a happy choice.

Of course, you can observe the animalistic aspects of human behavior practically anywhere as long as you are exposed to a steady stream of people. Why is a CPA practice so great for people watching? Because CPAs observe people going after money. As a CPA, I am exposed to people groveling and clawing after filthy lucre. Is there anything that magnifies the facets of human nature more than the pursuit of money? Of course not. Mankind's traits, characteristics, defects, and strengths, they are all amplified when money is involved.

Remember, though, I did not enter the CPA rat race just to observe people's behavior. I originally became an accountant to make money myself. What has watching others deal with their financial affairs got to do with that?

Well, it occurred to me that observing and analyzing business people might teach me something useful. If I could discern a difference between those who were successful and those who were not, perhaps I could copy the successful ones and become financially successful myself. In other words, perhaps some common denominators exist peculiar to prosperous people, and perhaps these traits are not totally dependent upon inherited characteristics. Maybe some are behavioral in nature. If so, then it might be possible to adopt techniques or systems or formulas that imitate whatever it is that makes successful people successful.

This idea has caused me to do more over the years than just account for clients' money. In addition to my duties as a CPA, I have spent considerable time observing people, sizing up their approach to things, and evaluating the effectiveness of their behavior. What makes them tick and their businesses click? Or stop and flop, as the case may be.

I am the first to admit that these observations are not scientific activity. Because they are based upon personal experience rather than scientific analysis, they are anecdotal in nature. You have to remember, though, that when it comes to telling anecdotes, I have considerable material to draw upon. Over the years, several thousand business clients have passed through my doors. And these have not been trivial or casual contacts. For the most part, they have involved in-depth relationships. So, even though my conclusions are based upon personal experience and intuition, they are much more than armchair instinct.

Well, how about it? What insights have I gained? Is there really a system or formula for acquiring wealth? Yes, there is something different about people who have achieved great economic success. What sets them apart isn't always readily apparent, because the characteristics I have in mind don't necessarily involve outward personality traits. Successful people represent a variety of personalities, but, generally speaking, they do share some basic attributes. We will review these characteristics in chapters to come.

What else have I learned? It was a big surprise discovering just how hard it is to become rich. Making serious money is exceedingly difficult. I never expected it to be easy, of course, but I never imagined it would be as will-of-the-wispy as it seems, either. Of all the business people I've known over the years, guess how many ultimately became millionaires? A couple of dozen or so, give or take a few, depending upon where you draw the line. Twenty-four out of several thousand? That is less than one percent!

Mind you, a number of others became reasonably affluent, but as far as people who really hit it big are concerned, we are talking a small number. And you have to remember the population they are drawn from is a select group. People seeking the services of a CPA firm are normally above average in intelligence and ambition.

Does my get-rich figure of less than one percent seem low? Well, it isn't. The percentage of millionaires found among the greater adult population is a fraction of that among my clients.

Why is it that getting rich is so difficult? I have often pondered that question in the wee small hours of the night. Obviously, many roadblocks are in the way. Otherwise, many more would reach wealth's destination. Years of observing people as a CPA have given me some answers. The chapters that follow will discuss the barriers that exist and explain how to overcome them.

Social scientists say that several factors correlate closely with an individual's economic success, such as the economic status of one's family as well as one's educational background and cultural heritage. In other words, being well-bred, good-looking, and smart helps. But that only partially accounts for how well a person does in the business world jungle. There is a large, unexplained, subjective component that social scientists have dubbed the "X factor." Many years of working with diverse business people have taught me what the X factor is all about. These are the sorts of things that will be discussed throughout this book.

I hear you out there! You're saying: "Okay, smart guy, if you know so much, how come you aren't rich?" First of all, it's too late for me. Many of the conclusions and understandings presented here came late in life. Furthermore, although I'm not filthy rich, I'm reasonably comfortable, thank you, and at this stage in life that's enough. At my age, I don't want the hassles and work and effort it takes to implement the things that will be described later. But you, dear reader, may yet be young enough and energetic enough and ambitious enough and motivated enough to go for it. If so, this book is for you, because it will help you get there.

But that isn't the point. Fabricating a fortune is not the objective. Because one other attribute of being rich also surprised me. You know something? Rich people are not any happier than you or I! In terms of human happiness, one does not need vast wealth in order to succeed in life.

Therefore, this book is not a get-rich-quick fix. Instead, it is about becoming successful, which by my definition means acquiring enough affluence to feel secure, happy, and self-fulfilled. Helping you achieve this state of affairs through running a small business is what this book is all about.

The point is, personal attributes of those who accumulate great wealth are equally appropriate for those with more modest goals. Regardless of the techniques you apply or approaches you adopt, whether gleaned from this book or others, your chances of becoming a Daddy (or Mama) Warbucks billionaire are slim. But that doesn't mean you will have failed. If, through conscious altering of your attitudes and behavior, you wind up further down the economic road than you would otherwise, how can you have failed?

So, here for your benefit are the things that I and many of my clients have learned over the years, the things we wish we had known when starting out in business. May you profit from them.

CHAPTER 2

COURTING LADY LUCK

Chance favors the prepared mind.
Russell Doolittle, biochemist

Obviously, luck is a big factor in the outcome of a small business. Anyone with five minutes of business experience knows that. Sometimes luck is a crusher. After a successful career in advertising and public relations, one of my clients decided to go into the movie-making business. That business is, of course, a difficult nut to crack. My client spent several years accumulating scripts, making the right contacts, and seeking investors. Not surprisingly, the hardest part was finding a financial angel to front production costs. After much time and effort and talking his brains out, he finally attracted a wealthy investor to back his first movie. He energetically set about refining the script, creating a budget, lining up actors and directors, and making all of the necessary logistic arrangements. When everything was set, he visited his investor and told him they were in position to proceed.

"Fine," said the investor, "I will call my banker Monday and have the money transferred to your company's account." After all my client's hard work, planning, and disappointments, it appeared things were finally going to pay off. That was Friday. On Sunday, I received a frantic phone call at home. It was my client, and he was so broken up he could barely speak. "Ted," he said, his voice cracking, "my investor just had a heart attack and died!"

Needless to say, my client's financing expired along with his investor's last breath. Out of all of the days in the investor's life, why did his death happen at that particular time? Why couldn't fate have delayed it just 24 hours, after investing in my client's business?

The point is, there is such a thing as blind, dumb luck, and often it overpowers everything else. Sometimes the best laid plans get laid low. As much as we would like to think we are masters of our own fate, we are often bullied by extraneous forces.

Granted, we are subject to outrageous fortune's slings and arrows. So what? By definition we can't change our luck. So why talk about it?

First, it is important that small business entrepreneurs recognize the existence of luck, because many in the world of commerce don't. Most notably, consultants, economists, and investment gurus. So, when people offer you advice, whether paid for or gratuitous, it is essential that you evaluate their counsel with the notion of uncertainty firmly in mind.

Second, appreciating the influence of luck helps avoid the trap of linear thinking. The famous jurist Judge Lord Shaw once wrote: "Causation is not a chain, but a net. At each point, influences, forces and events, precedent and simultaneous, meet; and the radiations from each point extend infinitely."

This is an elegant statement of the proposition that our lives are tweaked constantly by an infinite network of events. As a consequence, figuring out what causes what is risky business. Modern science has a term for this concept. It is called the chaos theory, and it applies to the mundane affairs of humankind as well as to scientific happenings. Chaos theory says that much of life is nonlinear, so, even when we know most of the factors affecting a situation, only rarely can we accurately predict outcomes. Too many factors are pulling and tugging in diverse directions. Yet, business people continually blunder into the intellectual trap of trying to establish straight-line, X-causes-Y, linear chains of cause and effect. If you depend upon linear thinking in the business world, you teeter on a narrow ledge. One puff of wind or one loose stone dumps you into the abyss.

An interesting example of how off-the-wall factors can screw up linear predictions is the history of the price of gold. The guru of gold, Howard J. Ruff, sent out a newsletter back in 1981 ballyhooing his prediction of an imminent, spectacular rise in the price of gold: "Gold will be at least $550 by early 1982, and $2,000 in this decade," huffed and puffed Ruff.

His reasoning was simple and deceptively appealing:

1. The federal government is committed to enormous levels of spending.

2. Government spending causes inflation.

3. Inflation causes gold prices to rise.

Ergo, as any fool can plainly see, gold prices will skyrocket. So, advised Ruff, buy gold now before ignorant nonreaders of my newsletter wise up. Ten years later, the 1980s cheerfully cake-walked to a close, with gold prices still mired at the $300 to $400 level. Ruff, along with like-minded colleagues, was embarrassingly wrong. What happened?

Ruff assumed that history inevitably repeats itself in stuck-in-a-rut fashion. A classic example of misplaced reliance on naive extrapolation and simplistic reductionism, the idiot parents of conjecture. *Extrapolation*—To predict the future by projecting from experience. (For example, anticipating the next pitch to be a fast ball because that is what the last two pitches were.) *Reductionism*—To explain complex phenomena in terms of single causes. (For example, claiming you won the baseball game because you ate Wheaties for breakfast.) *Conjecture*—To infer from defective or presumptive evidence. (For example, making assumptions based upon dumb conclusions like the ones above.) All factors at the time of his prediction indicated that inflation would run rampant in the 1980s—assuming, that is, that everything stayed the same, as though we were caught in a time warp.

Since Ruff's prediction, inflation has been an anemic shadow of its former self. No one back in 1981 could have anticipated our government capable of footwork fancy enough to curb inflation and endure stupendous deficits at the same time. No one back then could have predicted the collapse of OPEC's price-fixing oil cartel, or the cut-rate sale of oil by Iran and Iraq to finance their internecine war, or the Chernobyl nuclear power plant disaster, which caused the Soviets to liquidate gold reserves to finance ruined property and crops. And who could have foreseen the breakthroughs in mining technology that dramatically increased gold production? How about reduced defense spending brought about by the collapse of communism in eastern Europe?

Remember, though, that causation is a net rather than a chain. Diverse, seemingly unrelated factors can make the wisest of predictions go awry. Does all of this make life seem uncontrollable? A sink-hole of fatalism? A black hole of despair? Don't give up hope yet. There is a rational way to deal with fate.

Although we can't completely eliminate luck from our lives, we can control its influence. According to chaos theory, the things that happen to an individual may be unpredictable, but they aren't completely random, either. By standing back and looking at life from the proper perspective, patterns appear. The secret is to concentrate on being prepared ahead of time for a diverse range of happenings. By planning in advance for a broad spectrum of prospective events, you will reduce the impact that happenstance has on the outcome, and you will be in a better position to take advantage of fortuitous situations should they arise. As Michael LeBoeuf of the University of New Orleans put it, "Luck is opportunity meeting preparation."

Mind you, from time to time things are bound to happen that could not reasonably be anticipated and could not be forestalled even if foreseen. But in the main and up to a point, the more you prepare and plan and rehearse and visualize, the more good luck you will have. Over an extended period of time, preparation and good fortune go hand in hand. That, basically, is what this book is all about. Preparing you ahead of time so you can avoid the potholes and washed-out bridges of business life and find the yellow-brick road to success instead.

Another reason to talk about luck is that it is vital we be conscious of its existence when it grabs the steering wheel. Although we can't influence luck in the literal sense, what we can alter is our attitude toward it. Failure to appreciate when outcomes are attributable to blind, dumb luck can have disastrous long-range consequences. This applies equally whether we are talking good luck or bad luck.

I frequently see clients who attribute success to their personal skills and wisdom when, in fact, they just got lucky. The danger is in becoming too confident of one's prowess and infallibility. "Don't question my decisions, I know what the hell I am doing. After all, I made a hundred thou' last year." Like an arrogant flea on a prize-winning dog, such people think the applause is for them when good fortune causes the right dog to walk in front of their last jump.

It is surprising how often you see that attitude, but perhaps not so surprising after all when you consider the content of the pop psychology seminars so popular these days. There is a folklore mythology being marketed energetically that often is applied to business affairs. The philosophy is if you are determined and have goals and have the right attitude and are positive and follow the right formulas and pay me 500 bucks for this seminar/book/set of tapes, you will be successful, no doubt about it.* It is buttressed by the pop-psychology notion that you can be in charge of your life and choose what you do and what happens to you. Ordinarily, this might seem a harmless, albeit simplistic, philosophy, but it can get you into hot water if you believe in it too deeply.

A contractor client, through a slap-happy set of serendipitous circumstances, had the good fortune to make a killing on a couple of large back-to-back jobs. His new-found success affected him profoundly. In his own eyes, he became infallible. Nothing he said or did from that point on was susceptible to criticism, constructive or otherwise. He henceforth obligated his company to an incredibly ambitious expansion scheme. Nothing anybody said caused him even to pause for reflection, let alone dissuade him. "Don't bother me, I'm on a roll," was his motto, as he committed his company to grandiose projects far outside the range of his experience. To finance the expansion, he dangerously overextended. This time, Lady Luck left him holding the bag. A series of fiscal reversals transformed his business empire into bankruptcy bait. Within a few years' time, all the economic success he previously had created came crashing down around his ears.

What was the cause of his pratfall? He failed to recognize that his previous success had been heavily favored by good fortune more than anything else. He assumed he was successful because his unique foresight and intelligence enabled him to see through walls. As a consequence, he put far too much reliance on his supposed infallible judgment.

On the other hand, I have seen clients hurt themselves because they failed to recognize the existence of bad luck. There was, for example, the contractor whose company experienced a string of unfortunate, unforeseen disasters on a very large job. The result was an impossible financial

---

*Some get-rich-quick gurus have fallen on hard times lately. Albert J. Lowery is probably the best known, having written the widely distributed *How You Can Become Financially Independent by Investing in Real Estate* and *How to Become Successful Owning Your Own Business*. In a classic case of do as I say and not as I do, Lowery subsequently had to file for personal bankruptcy.

situation. My client's partners did the logical thing. They abandoned the sinking ship. The fact that this behavior is associated with rats didn't bother them. Emitting a few squeaks, they left the corporation and found employment elsewhere. My client, however, was made of sterner stuff. By gawd, this situation wasn't going to lick him. He was going to see it through and bring his company back from the brink of ruin.

So he proceeded to spend some of the best years of his life nursing back to health what was essentially a terminally ill, bankrupt company. And I'll be darned if he didn't eventually do it, much to his credit. He ultimately paid all of his company's creditors. But what did he really get, after all was said and done, other than the satisfaction of a moral victory? In the end, he had a company with no credit because of its long history of slow pay. A company with no bonding capacity because of inadequate working capital. A company with tired, worn out equipment because no money was available for replacements. And much hard work, worry, and no financial rewards.

How much better off would he have been had he recognized it wasn't his fault the original job went bad? That it was no reflection on him but merely a case of being hit with some very bad luck, which is a fact of life in the construction business? It isn't always possible to figure out what is going on underground. The moral is: If you are losing a tug-of-war with a tiger, give him the rope before he munches up your arm. You can always find another rope.

We are not always completely responsible as individuals for the outcome of things as complex as business ventures, so don't take what happens too personally, either in terms of credit or blame. Develop the wisdom to discern when things are the result of your own input and guidance and when they are due to the convergence of unforeseen sets of circumstances. Being right for the wrong reasons, in other words, can backfire in the long run.

Finally, don't fall into the justice trap. How many times, oh Lord, have I heard the lament, "But it just isn't fair!"? Where is it written that life is supposed to be fair? If you get dumped on, don't waste your time waiting for justice. Some people become totally immobilized when things go sour and don't work out as hoped. These are loser behaviors guaranteed to make you miss out on future opportunities.

THE SECOND COMING OF THE WOOLLY MAMMOTH

So, lift up your head and take a walk in the sun, Bunky! After all, it's a privilege just being alive, so how can life owe us anything? Have the grace and grit to take things as they come and you may be surprised how much "luck" you have.

CHAPTER 3

FACING REALITY

The life of a man in this world is like the life of a fly in a room filled with 100 boys, each armed with a fly-swatter. H. L. Mencken

How does a small business entrepreneur become successful in a world obviously filled with difficulties? Books on small business normally contain extensive shopping lists of causes thought to account for small business failures. They put forth brilliantly insipid revelations, blaming such things as bad management, inadequate financing, insufficient sales volume, and high costs. Thank you, Dick Tracy.

In the last analysis, business failures are attributable to only three causes, or some combination thereof. These causes are:

1. Bad luck

2. Failure to recognize reality

3. Failure to respond rationally to reality

Bumping into a tree in the dark of night is bad luck. The fact that tree trunks have hard surfaces is reality. Kicking the hell out of the tree and breaking your toe is not responding rationally to reality. Beyond the factor of bad luck, all of the supposed causes for business failures distill down to a failure to recognize and respond rationally to reality. That is about the size of it.

The world of small business is filled with tree kickers. Don't kick the tree; get a chain saw and cut it down. You are almost always guaranteed success if you consistently do just two things: first, realistically discern the true facts surrounding your situation and, second, react to those facts in a rational manner. In other words, wake up and smell the espresso.

Realistically discern the facts? One of my clients paid three times too much for a restaurant operation. There was no way the restaurant could earn enough to make his payments. That fact could easily be demonstrated. Yet, the client struggled, struggled, and struggled, refusing to recognize that he had struck a bad bargain. He fell back on the false comfort of ignoring unpleasant reality.

Respond rationally to reality? For five years in a row, a client lost an enormous amount of money operating an art gallery as a side operation to her profitable other line of business. Recognizing reality was not her problem. She was painfully aware the gallery was a black hole for losing money. This she readily acknowledged. Yet, pride, procrastination, and emotional considerations kept her from closing down the gallery. She tried to drown reality with irrational responses.

Recognizing reality and acting rationally to reality may be slam-dunk advice, but it is difficult advice to carry out because it involves abstract concepts. Translating abstract ideas and generalizations into overt action is always tough because we have to overcome some psychological predispositions. Human nature binds and blinds us. We operate day-to-day, tied to a tangle of psychological defense mechanisms. At the same time, we are heavily influenced by the exotic baggage of emotional impulses we carry around. And lurking deep down in our mental cellars is a complex assortment of vague instincts and powerful drives. All function independent of one another while thumbing their collective noses at the neocortex part of the brain. Mix the whole mess together and you have that wonderful hodgepodge of contradictions—human nature.

Because of human nature, our psychological defense systems come well equipped with filters that screen incoming sensory information toward a bias in favor of what we would like to see and hear rather than the bare bones of unpleasant reality. As Stephen Jay Gould remarked, "We observe according to preset categories and often cannot 'see' what stares us in the face." In addition, information going out of our bodies is filtered as well. We learn quickly in life that the wisest course is to portray only what we want the outside world to know rather than our true thoughts and feelings. Perhaps that is why most people have about 24 different facial expressions as children but wind up with only six as adults.

Besides our internal predisposition to distort, we have another problem to overcome. Even with a realistic outlook, it is virtually impossible to figure out totally what is true and what is not. We are constantly bombarded by incredible amounts of information. Some of it is accurate, some is baloney, and much is a mixed bag of both. Most of the time we are forced to make decisions before we have a chance to find out the true mixture. Acquiring reliable information is always difficult because there are lots of "leg pullers" out there. To make matters worse, the barrage of information that assaults our senses is almost always incomplete. There are enormous gaps in the stream of information that comes to us, and continuity is usually lacking. It isn't always the lies people tell that hurt; it is often what they don't tell us that gives us grief.

Sounds hopeless, doesn't it? With all the factors stacked against it, why bother discussing the achievement of a realistic outlook? Because a brightly lighted tunnel lies within the paradox. The difficulty itself represents opportunity. Remember, everyone else has the same problem. We share a universal experience in this regard, which means that coping with life is a matter of relativity rather than absolutes. We don't have to create the perfect situation in our business lives, because no one else ever does, either. The objective, therefore, is not complete rationality. Instead of trying to be a totally rational person, all we really need to do is be a bit more rational than most other people.

What we are after are strategies that do nothing more than give us an edge—attitudes and behaviors that weigh the odds our way, that increase our chances for success. From the standpoint of what is practical, this can be done. The trouble is, achieving this means we must often perform in ways that are unnatural to us—like wild bears that are trained to dance in the circus. To be successful, we must adopt strategies and behaviors that conflict with our true natures. This requires a heavy investment in emotional labor and is why most entrepreneur wannabees are daydreamers rather than dreammakers.

How many people, for example, enjoy dunning customers to collect tardy receivables? Yet, to be successful, it has to be done. How many enjoy being continually nice to people they don't really like? Yet, if they want to keep customers, this also must be done. People can achieve greater financial success if they are willing to be thoroughly cold-blooded when pursuing business affairs. Not cold-blooded toward others, but rather with respect to themselves. They should be cold-blooded as to their own natural inclinations and personal proclivities.

Do you want to dance in the circus or not? You'd better decide, because success in small business means talking yourself into spending more time than you'd like doing things you don't particularly like to do. Inhibit your proclivities and override your emotions? How can that be accomplished? Stay tuned. I believe there are answers to this dilemma.

As a recording device, human memory is a fragile thing—part fact, part fancy. It is distorted by the presence of strong wishes and desires, it is easily contaminated by the arrival of new information, and it tends to deteriorate under stress.

PART TWO

PERSONAL ATTRIBUTES OF

SMALL BUSINESS WINNERS

CHAPTER 4

AN OPEN LETTER TO

WOULD-BE ENTREPRENEURS

Lack of charisma can be fatal.   Jenny Holzer

Dear Entrepreneur to Be:

I understand your nervousness as you contemplate going out on your own. Starting a business is a scary proposition. But don't feel intimidated. An important attribute for achieving success in business is adroitness in dealing with people. That is a quality that can be acquired if not already possessed. Irrespective of everything else, you at least have that much going for you.

The reason people skills are so important is that business is not an abstract activity. The business world is a living, breathing thing composed of interactions between human beings. It is the interactions that are key. There are many people walking around with technical ability and intelligence and good ideas, but the ones most likely to succeed financially are those adept at dealing with others, those who can sell themselves to others and get people to like them.

The old saw, "It's who you know that counts," is only partially right. Knowing people (*networking* is the contemporary term) isn't enough. A network of acquaintances is of consequence only if you have personal influence over your contacts. That is why social grooming is as important for humans as it is for chimpanzees.

Does this make it sound like a personality contest out there? Of course it does, because in effect it is. That is why it is said that an ounce of image is worth a pound of performance. This merely reflects human nature. If you don't believe it, ask the people in charge of presidential campaigns.

Most people starting out really don't understand how to make money. The basic principle is that you have to achieve leverage; you have to discover a way to multiply your personal efforts. Most of us can't justify being paid very much for an hour's worth of our time (unless, of course, one happens to be a superstar). And there are only so many hours in a day, so you can't catch up by putting in more hours. Making money going one-on-one is hard, if not impossible.

This means you must somehow make your own time be the focus of a multiplier effect. Whatever work you do must lever a small amount of effort into a large ultimate effect. There are several ways this can be done in the world of economics. One is to sell expensive products. Sales commissions normally are calculated on a percentage basis, so the fee you earn is based on the size of your sale. Which is why real estate can be so rewarding. Usually, it doesn't take any more time to sell a $1,000,000 piece of property than it does a $100,000 parcel. But a five percent sales commission earns you ten times as much in the same amount of time— $50,000 versus $5,000. I know several people who have made a great deal of money because of this principle.

A variation is to sell low-cost items in bulk quantities. The commission for selling one candy bar is about one peanut. But a million one-dollar candy bars equals a million dollar sale and enough commission peanuts to feed a herd of elephants. I know someone who makes a ton of money peddling candy bars, but he doesn't deal in individual bars. He is a middleman, a manufacturer's representative who sells large quantities to supermarket chains.

Another leverage example is being president or top executive of a large organization. I used to do the taxes for the president of a very large bank in town. This man's salary was, in his own words, obscene. Bank presidents make incredible salaries, not because their personal time is so valuable but, rather, because they control large numbers of people and large amounts of money. By being at the apex of a pyramid and assuming the responsibility this entails, they are entitled to a little bit of every productive unit beneath them. Because of the large numbers involved, this means big bucks on their paychecks.

The classic way to multiply your efforts, though, is with other people's money, commonly referred to as O.P.M. (See Chapter 24 for further discussion of the principle of O.P.M.) In other words, borrow money from investors, partners, banks, friends, or "pigeons" to use for investing. If you work it right, you may be able to get away with investing only a small amount of your own money while retaining most of the profits. Suppose you borrow 90 percent of the total investment needed at 10 percent interest and the business venture itself earns 15 percent. After paying interest costs on the borrowed money, the venture is left with only six percent $(.15 - [.10 \times .90] = .06)$. But look at the return you have on the amount that you yourself invested—60 percent $(.06/.10 = .60)$! Slightly better, wouldn't you say, than the 15 percent you would have earned if you yourself had provided all of the investment money?

I have a friend who became rich because he was able to successfully coax money out of investors. He started out as I did in public accounting but was not a very good CPA. As a matter of fact, it took him a number of tries to pass the CPA exam. But he had a very potent quality. He was a popular person with lots of friends, a real character whose gift of gab caused people to enjoy being around him. So he left public accounting and started putting together real estate investments using his broad base of acquaintances as investors. For putting the deals together, he obtained free interests in the ventures as well as management fees. As a result, he didn't need much money of his own and was able to leverage himself into an incredible position that, with lucky timing, ultimately resulted in his becoming a millionaire.

Now, notice what the foregoing examples have in common, besides the principle of leverage. They involve four separate paths to becoming rich, but each one required strong people skills to get there. All of the successes I've cited were carried on the wings of charisma and effective personal skills.

You don't become a successful real estate salesperson, manufacturer's representative, bank president, or investment advisor without people skills. Of course, a certain amount of technical ability is necessary as well. But the amount of technical ability needed is not out of the ordinary, whereas the amount of personality is.

I hope the foregoing thoughts are useful in mulling over your future. You very definitely can learn to swim in the economic world if you train your personality to use the right strokes. And if you manage to find a situation in which you can use leverage as an income multiplier, you stand as good a chance as anyone of becoming financially successful.

Life out there on your own in the small business swamp appears scary, I know. But once you get your feet wet, you will find it a more comfortable environment than it appears at a distance. Best of all, if you manage to keep your sense of humor, it can even turn out to be a hoot.

Good luck to you.

CHAPTER 5

ARE YOU AN ALPHA?

He was a yelling, wiry, malevolent, sneevily, snively
Bully who had quelled all insurgents for miles around. I
did not know one kid who was not afraid of Dill, mainly
because Dill was truly aggressive. This kind of aggression
later on in life is often called "Talent" or "Drive."
Jean Shepherd

What is the single most important ingredient necessary for success in small business? You may be surprised to learn that intelligence is not the answer. A high degree of intelligence is useful in small business as in nearly every other field of endeavor. So is personality, perseverance, high energy level, resourcefulness, and sound judgment. All of these qualities are mighty handy to have, but none is an absolute prerequisite.

There is one characteristic, however, that is absolutely essential: aggression! If you are going to make a go of things financially, you've got to be aggressive! Small business people cover the spectrum as far as personality traits and mental capacities go, but the successful ones I've known all have one common characteristic. They've been aggressive as hell! I don't mean physical pugnaciousness. The aggression I refer to is the general, overall desire to dominate, the urge to compete and prevail, the drive to impose one's will upon others. Those lacking a high degree of this characteristic don't, as a rule, do well in the world of small business.

This might seem a questionable assertion to make, since psychologists claim that cooperation rather than competitiveness more likely leads to success in our culture. (See, for example, Alfie Kohn's *No Contest: The Case Against Competition*.) It's a matter of context. Studies indicating that cooperation is the key to success involve analysis of behavior between individuals within a group, such as the situation in academic and big business environments. Small business is a different ball game. It involves behavior of an individual toward outsiders. Nurturing a cooperative spirit among one's employees is not inconsistent with going tooth-and-fang against the company's competitors. You'll find it described in Deuteronomy.

Small business owners are typically hemmed in by competitive pressures. They live in a snake pit of conflict. Their competitors want their customers, their customers want lower prices, their suppliers want higher prices, their landlords want more rent, their employees want better fringe benefits, the IRS wants more taxes, and the government wants compliance with more bureaucratic red tape. Practically everyone with whom a small business person deals wants a concession. So, for a small business owner, a heavy dose of aggressiveness is a valuable asset.

But keep in mind what I mean by *aggression*. When I use this term, I am referring to the motivational sense of the word, not to its overt connotation. Being aggressive in business does not mean that you go around looking for asses to kick. Nor does it mean that you should adopt "Read my lips" as your favorite expression. It does mean being energized by the internal pressures that aggressive impulses generate, but expressed in a socially acceptable format.

A scientific description of this lies in the biological concept of the so-called *alpha*. Biologists have long observed the existence within most animal populations of certain dominant individuals known as alphas. Alphas are characterized by aggressive, domineering behavior. They are the ones that end up with the best food, the choicest mates, and the most desirable territories. Whatever the popular status symbol may be, alphas are the ones that corner the market.

Next comes a group of individuals known as *betas*. Betas compete and strive for dominance also, but unfortunately (for them), they don't quite have what it takes. Consequently, betas become dominated by alphas.

Finally, there are the *omegas*. Omegas are life's perpetual losers—the Charlie Browns of the species. Omegas are the ones that have lost so often they have dropped out. They don't even bother trying to compete anymore.

These three categories have been observed in practically every animal species, from fish to rats to monkeys to humans. Nobody knows yet what causes an individual to be predisposed towards "alphaness." Important ingredients seem to be virility, courage, energy, strength, confidence, ambition, and luck. Among humans, one thing is for sure, alphas make awfully good business people!

Most of the successful small business people I've known have been pretty tough characters, gutsy, aggressive, self-assured, and competitive. Definitely alphas. The stress and strain of striving and competing doesn't seem to bother them. As a matter of fact, they appear to thrive on the rigors of the business world. Alphas are known to be much less prone to heart attacks and ulcers than betas.

So, if you think you possess alpha qualities, going into business for yourself is probably a good idea. Owning your own business may give you the chance to be the competitor that by nature you are. On the other hand, if you are a beta or an omega, take my advice and forget it. If you are a beta or an omega and go into business for yourself, you probably will end up being unsuccessful and miserable and will increase your chances of developing a stress-related disease besides.

Again, let there be no misunderstanding of my terminology. By *aggression*, I do not mean physical or hostile behavior. Overt, naked aggression in a modern civilized society backfires. One of my favorite episodes in the "Peanuts" comic strip shows Lucy berating Charlie Brown for not standing up to one of his playmates who had wronged him. Lucy asks, "Why don't you hit him in the mouth, Charlie Brown?" Charlie Brown replies, "Because I have observed when you hit somebody in the mouth, there is a tendency for them to hit you back."

Very astute, Charlie Brown. So the term *aggression*, as used here, means the urge to dominate and prevail rather than kung fu combativeness. A euphemistic word for this characteristic is *assertiveness*, as used in the assertiveness training programs that were so popular several years back. It is interesting to note that assertiveness training programs now have a qualifier in their course descriptions. They are currently called "responsible" assertiveness programs. The emphasis is away from direct confrontation, toward mutuality. In other words, the strategy is to get your own way but to do it in a manner that ensures the integrity and self-respect of others.

The point is, possessing a heavy dose of aggression is desirable, but, at the same time, you should express it in ways that won't backfire. Remember the old saying, "You can't persuade and antagonize at the same time." If you try to macho-man everybody into submission, you will be shunned and no one will deal with you. The only time you can kick somebody around with impunity these days is when all the power is on your side, which is a rare situation in our society. Even pet owners are subject to cruelty-to-animal laws.

So, in expressing and carrying out your aggressive impulses, you must use socially acceptable means. You have to be sneaky when applying aggression in our culture, because there are strict rules as to how the game is played. But, as a wise old businessman once told me, there are many different ways to fight. The essential thing is that the urge to fight exists.

Occasionally in business you'll encounter a totally unreasonable person—a pig-headed, obnoxious jerk. Avoid this sort of person like the plague. Doing business with yahoos always backfires in the end. Invariably you'll lose with such people, because they play the game using a unique set of rules—their own.

CHAPTER 6

THE MANY FACES OF IQ

Definition of a smart ass? Someone who can sit on an ice cream cone and tell you what flavor it is.   Anonymous

It surprised me to discover how small a role intelligence plays in business. When I first entered the business world, I assumed exceptionally bright people were the ones making all the money. I expected successful business people to be big in the smarts department and the unsuccessful ones to be the dummies. It was a revelation to learn this is not the case.

My prior experience had been 18 years of school and college, where academic achievements get the recognition and rewards. In an academic environment, it is the people who have high IQs that are successful. I automatically transferred that order of things to the world of commerce.

Although the brightest kids may get the highest marks in school, the same pattern doesn't hold up when hustling a living. Straight "A" students don't automatically get straight "A"s in business. There, scores are kept differently, money is used for grades, and your balance sheet is your report card.

Now, I am not saying it doesn't help to be smart in a business setting. Of course it does. But you don't have to be a card-carrying member of Mensa to succeed. As a matter of fact, high intellect may actually be a detriment. Intelligent people tend to become confused and indecisive when bombarded by too many facts. Double-dome types see three sides to every question and are inclined toward getting hung up gathering and analyzing data and relating everything to the philosophical meanings of life. So, if I introduced you to the successful business people I've known, you'd probably say, "Well, they are smart people, all right, but they certainly aren't geniuses."

This seems to be a common observation. I have a friend, for example, who is brilliant. Those of us who know him always expected he would set the world on fire. He has been successful, certainly, but, on the other hand, hasn't wound up anywhere near as prosperous as we thought he would. A few years ago, in a moment of reflection, my friend made a rueful remark, "You know something, Frost? I've discovered that brains are a dime a dozen in the business world." Very true. But this fact has always been a puzzlement to me. Somehow, it always seemed that intelligence should be a stronger factor in business.

Recently, a theory has been advanced that sheds light on the subject. A group of psychologists have attacked the concept of IQ—more specifically, the IQ test. They argue there is no such thing as intelligence, per se. In their view, no single human quality exists that can be labeled intelligence. Therefore, IQ tests are misleading because they measure only a narrow range of intellectual skills—namely, those important in an academic setting.

One of the leading proponents of this new school of thought is a psychologist named Howard Gardner, who teaches at Harvard University. Gardner claims seven different varieties of intelligence exist that are autonomous (that is, independent of one another). Gardner says IQ tests measure only two of the seven types of intelligence—verbal and math/logic intelligence.

This is an intriguing concept because it opens up the possibility that there are numerous ways of being smart. As a matter of fact, two of Gardner's categories do show up in successful small business people, and neither one of these is measured in an IQ test. They are:

1. Adroitness in dealing with others, which Gardner calls inTERpersonal skill

2. Knowledge of one's self, which Gardner calls inTRApersonal skill

This begins to explain why people we normally think of as being highly intelligent don't necessarily turn out to be the whiz-bangs we thought they would when they enter the business world.

THE SECOND COMING OF THE WOOLLY MAMMOTH

Once outside of a classroom setting, other intelligences come into play that standard achievement tests don't measure. Some of these skills relate to success in business and don't surface in a prominent way until a person sallies forth into the real world of dog-eat-dog and devil-take-the-leftovers. Since these forms of intelligence are completely independent of skills emphasized in school, grade point averages are not a reliable predictor of entrepreneurial success.

This is why abstract intelligence in and of itself often doesn't accomplish much in business. Success in small business involves much more than that. To succeed, you must integrate your intellectual components with practical experience and utilize the resultant wisdom to interact with your environment. The process involves going from analytical thinking to creative thinking to street-smart manipulation of your environment. You learn these things in the back alleys of life rather than in the classroom. (For more information on nonacademic intelligence, see Howard Gardner's *Frames of Mind: The Theory of Multiple Intelligences*.)

So, take heart, all of you ex-"C" students out there. There may be facets to your intelligence that haven't been measured yet. Who knows, some day you may even wind up being vice-president of the United States.

CHAPTER 7

PEOPLE RADAR

I sniff and guess. I pick things out of the wind and air.   Carl Sandburg

People who claim extrasensory powers suggest that mental telepathy existed as a means of communication before our ancestors acquired the power of speech. Psychics claim that all humans possess extrasensory faculties, to varying degrees. In the cold light of day, this sounds like spooky, far out stuff. But it does tie in to one of the subjects mentioned in the previous chapter—interpersonal intelligence.

Howard Gardner's concept of interpersonal intelligence is the ability to notice and make distinctions between other individuals as to meanings and motives. Sometimes it is referred to as *people radar.* Those persons who have a high level of people radar can discern moods and intentions of others, even when the person being observed plays it cool and tries to cover up his or her true feelings.

The results may seem like mental telepathy, but there is a scientific explanation. Scientists attribute this capacity to highly developed skills for reading imperceptible physiological and psychological clues. It is well documented that the conscious part of our brain selectively filters information and stimuli. Censorship is its *modus operandi.*

At the same time, the subconscious mind operates like a "free speech" society: it lets everything in, including subliminal messages. Interpersonal intelligence involves the ability to forage among the dumping grounds of the subconscious mind for clues and messages that may have been overlooked at the conscious level. It's an awesome and sometimes scary talent. After watching individuals who possess high levels of people radar in action, I've developed great respect for their "sixth-sense" abilities.

We all operate to a certain extent behind masks and facades. Particularly in the realm of business, where people often think of themselves as being engaged in a poker game. Those people in business who say what they really think are as rare as a forthright politician. Consequently, what an advantage it must be being able to figure out what others are really up to and to have some feel for the strength of their commitments. What a valuable asset it must be to have the aptitude to assess moods and motivations of others, to have the insight to predict their reactions and responses. I am sure that is why this attribute seems to exist to such a high degree in the successful business people I've known.

Several years ago, a hard-charging client of mine was in the throes of contemplating the purchase of another company to add to his family of enterprises. He asked me to accompany him to interview the target company's treasurer. The purpose of our call was to get a better feel for the company's operations and its financial position. The treasurer was very lucid and answered our questions in a straightforward manner. After the interview, as we were driving back to my client's office, he turned to me and asked, "What did you think of that guy, anyway?" I replied that I thought he had a good grasp of his company's affairs and seemed a very sharp fellow. Then my client said, "I think the S.O.B.'s been stealing."

"What!?" I exclaimed. "What in the world makes you think that?"

"I don't know," my client said, "but I just bet he has, that's all. I have a feeling he's been dipping into the till."

Three months later, the company's books were audited, and, guess what. Not only was the treasurer an embezzler, he had been embezzling on a big-league scale, to the tune of hundreds of thousands of dollars.

Now, how did my client know that? How could he possibly derive that conclusion from a two-hour interview? And remember, it wasn't an idle remark. He was certain of his convictions.

Was it a lucky guess? A wild hunch? Or a remarkable demonstration of intuitive powers? All I can say is that this particular client has demonstrated similar off-the-wall flashes of insight on other occasions (although perhaps none so dramatic as the incident I just described).

The point is, most successful business people have a high capacity for "reading" people, sometimes to a degree that is hard to explain. As Garfield the comic-strip cat once said when trying to explain why cats always manage to land on their feet, "We don't know how we does it, we just does it."

Isn't there some way that interpersonal skills can be developed? Sure. You can develop these skills by introspection. Listen to the voices within, harken to your subconscious murmurings. In other words, pay attention to your gut feel. Use your intuition.

Unfortunately, intuitive wisdom is usually thought of as being in the same category as home remedies for curing warts. Intuition has been looked down upon ever since the scientific method became established as the rational way to understand the world. It shouldn't be that way, really. There is much more to intuition than blind hunch. As Philip Goldberg wrote:

> Intuition is increasingly recognized as a natural mental faculty, a key element in discovery, problem solving, and decision making, a generator of creative ideas, a forecaster, a revealer of truth. . . . Those people who always seem to be in the right place at the right time, and for whom good things happen with uncanny frequency, are not just lucky; they have an intuitive sense of what to choose and how to act.

Many successful business people have vague feelings from time to time about particular matters that greatly influence their decisions. As a friend of mine sometimes remarks about such matters, "It doesn't pass the 'smell' test." Most people feel this way on occasion, but they may be bothered by such feelings. They usually brush them aside, because giving credence to them smacks of superstition.

How many times have you kicked yourself after something turned out contrary to your outward expectations by saying, "I *knew* I should/shouldn't have done that. I had a hunch it was the right/wrong thing to do." Yet, most people suppress such feelings when they arise because they cannot perceive a rational basis.

When I was younger, I operated that way myself. The many science courses I sat through during my schooling conditioned me to respect the logic of rational analysis. As a result, inductive and deductive reasoning became my bag. After graduating from college, I was convinced I could easily cut a swath through the crude world of business. All I needed for instant success was to apply the scientific method to business problems. It has been a good many years now since I first tried using that approach. Many's the time since I've lain awake at night trying to figure out why I fell flat on my *tokus* the preceding day. My conclusion? The wreckage of faulty logic lines the road to hell.

Logical reasoning, after all, is no big deal. Most people are capable of it on occasion, if they are given an underlying premise to start with. That, however, is the problem. All logical arguments must start from a foundation of fundamental premises or presuppositions. If these are false or subjectively warped, the whole train of logic that follows jumps the tracks.

Business people who analyze every situation logically tend to be over-confident of their reasoning. The beauty of their logic blinds them. All too often their reasoned analysis overlooks a faulty premise lurking in the bushes. Just when they have a situation all figured out, and after they have committed themselves to it—ZOT!—out jumps the faulty premise.

The point is, it is worthwhile to pay attention to your intuitive sense of things. Wisdom is not always capable of being articulated into words. Our minds are constantly churning at a subliminal level. So, if you have vague, uneasy feelings about some matters, don't be in such a hurry to brush them aside. Try to figure out why you feel that way. Consider what it is that brings out such feelings. It may be an emotional, irrational re-action, or it may be a manifestation of a psychological hang-up. On the other hand, your "sixth-sense" radar may be picking up vibrations not readily apparent on the surface. So, treat your intuition with respect. There is more common sense behind it than you realize.

CHAPTER 8

EGO POWER

We live amid surfaces and the true art of life is to learn to skate well on them. Ralph Waldo Emerson

One non-IQ intelligence that is characteristic of successful small business people is intrapersonal intelligence. This has to do with being in touch with your personal feelings and motives and being able to guide your behavior accordingly. It manifests itself this way: if I introduced you to one of my successful business acquaintances, you would likely notice a bloated ego filling the room; they all have powerful egos.

The word *ego* has bad connotations, but it is used here in a positive rather than a negative sense. Most successful business people have enormous amounts of self-confidence and self-esteem. They have a strong feeling for their abilities and for the quality of their judgments.

At the same time, they know their weaknesses. But their strong egos protect them from feeling threatened, so they don't hesitate to assign responsibility to others when they encounter some aspect of their affairs better handled by someone else. That's the essential difference between intrapersonal intelligence and pure unadulterated ego. Ego is a prominent component but only as raw material. Intrapersonal ego possesses perspective: it has gone to realism school.

You can readily see why strong ego is valuable in the business world. For starters, people who have strong egos don't worry about taking chances. They are not afraid to bet the family farm, because they know they can bounce back if things don't work out. They're not prisoners to security.

Second, a strong ego means you are less likely to be distracted by emotional feelings and conflicting interests of others. Egoists believe that "what's good for General Motors is good for the country." In other words, pursuing their own self-interests will indirectly benefit everyone else. This attitude helps resolve conflicts. It facilitates dealing with difficult matters, such as firing incompetent employees.

Third, strong ego contributes toward strong leadership and being able to elicit efforts from others. As the old Arab epigram goes:

> He who knows not and knows not that he knows not, is a fool. Avoid him.
> He who knows not but knows that he knows not, is ignorant. Instruct him.
> He who knows but knows not that he knows, is asleep. Awaken him.
> He who knows and knows that he knows, is a leader. Follow him.

Finally, a healthy ego is an important attribute of strong sales ability. Rejection is a fact of life in the business world. Being able to rebound after being whopped with rebuffs is enormously important. A healthy ego provides the necessary resiliency and resolve.

Of course, the key ingredient to all of this is not ego, per se, but intelligent ego. In other words, intrapersonal intelligence. Bombast and puffery not backed up by substance is an empty bag of wind and is easily deflated.

Muhammad Ali's legendary boxing skills were accompanied by an ego that wouldn't quit. As a member of the 1960 U.S. Olympic Games team, I had the opportunity to observe Ali firsthand. (His name was Cassius Clay back then.) The only thing faster than Ali's fists was his mouth. Ali's success caused a new style to evolve in boxing. Young, impressionable boxers started imitating Ali's "I am the greatest" oratory style. Obviously, they hoped it would do the same for them as it seemed to do for Ali. Braggadocio became a preliminary ritual to boxing bouts: "I'm gonna hit him so hard, when he wakes up, his clothes'll be outta style!"

Unfortunately for them, Ali's imitators found it easier to copy his verbosity than his boxing skills. As a result, their displays of boasting usually fell flat, in conformity with the flattened features that resulted from their lack of skill.

The difference is that Ali had a very high level of intrapersonal intelligence. Ali actually knew his abilities. His confidence was based upon reality, so his talk was not just wishful thinking or compensation for self doubts.

CHAPTER 9

SELF-IMAGE AND THE

CHARLIE BROWN SYNDROME

*William James (1842–1910) once said that the greatest
discovery of his time was that human beings could alter
their lives by altering their attitudes of minds.*

Some years ago, Maxwell Maltz wrote a popular self-help book entitled
Psycho-Cybernetics. Basically, the book promotes a power-of-positive-
thinking, pump-yourself-up philosophy of the same genre as books by
Norman Vincent Peale, Dale Carnegie, and others. Books of this ilk usually turn me off, because I believe them largely ineffectual. "Psycho-
babble" solutions to human personality problems have the bad habit of
wearing off as quickly as their application.

Psycho-Cybernetics, however, is written around an intriguing idea.
Maltz, a plastic surgeon by trade, expounds on the concept that people
develop a self-image early in life. He explains that once our minds
form this self-image, from that point on, regardless of its validity, we
act as though it were true. Maltz believes that our actions, feelings,
and behavior remain consistent with this self-image and that this causes
a caterpillars-crawling-around-the-rim-of-a-cup circle of self-fulfilling
behavior.

Maltz theorizes that people become uncomfortable psychologically
when their experiences conflict with their internal beliefs and attitudes.
In psychological terms, this phenomenon is sometimes referred to as

cognitive dissonance. People seek to relieve the discomfort of cognitive dissonance by striving to make events fit logically within their own perceptions. To accomplish this, they either rationalize internally or behave irrationally externally. Hence, the behavior pattern of people acting out negative self-images as opposed to living up to their true potential.

Maltz's concept has spawned a whole spate of self-help books and seminars aimed at altering one's self-image. (See, for example, Thomas A. Harris's *I'm O.K., You're O.K.: A Practical Guide to Transactional Analysis* or Dorothy Corkille Briggs's *Celebrate Yourself.*) Positive self-imagery is an "in" technique in sports as well as a hot topic for living in general. The idea is basically simple. Suppose that, as a youngster, you believed deep down inside you were a poor student. According to Maltz, your subsequent behavior would be consistent with this self-image in ways that would cause you to perform badly in school. You'd become a walking self-fulfilling prophecy. Neglecting your homework and losing interest in class would be your style because, after all, what's the use? Mediocre performance in school would reinforce your poor self-image, thereby setting you up, all cocked and loaded, ready for another round of poor performance.

What led Maltz to this conclusion was his experience as a plastic surgeon. After converting an ugly face into one that was "normal," Maltz observed that the patient often continued acting as though he or she were still ugly: the internal mind's eye continued to see the outer person as repulsive. The key to success, according to Maltz, is to perform psychological plastic surgery on one's self-image. *Psycho-Cybernetics* describes how to do this—how to change the view you have of yourself if you feel unworthy, inferior, undeserving, incapable, or otherwise negative.

There is definitely something to this. It has long been recognized that personal behavior is greatly influenced by the opinion people have of themselves. Self-esteem is an important ingredient in a person's overall effectiveness. A lousy self-image explains why some people are failure-prone and seemingly can't tolerate success. Extreme examples of this mechanism are those who are chronically accident-prone and people the cops call "victims walking around looking for a murderer."

Every once in a while, I come across a business person who repeatedly comes up to the brink of success or even crosses the threshold. Then, for some ridiculous reason, this same individual, after working hard and competently, proceeds to mess it up. The unusual thing about these types of people is that it is a constantly recurring pattern rather than an isolated incident.

There is the failure-prone sales person, for example, who works like mad putting together a big sale. Then, just when the deal is ready, for some reason or other he or she proceeds to bungle the order and lose out to a competitor. Or the business person who works diligently building up a sound, profitable business and then throws it away by goofing off, drinking, gambling, recklessly speculating—whatever destructive activities he or she can think of that will cause the business to fail.

Occasionally I am called upon to interview and hire accounting personnel for clients. Some applicants seem exceptionally well qualified. Their education, appearance, experience—all of their qualifications— look good except for one peculiar fact. They've had numerous previous jobs or been in numerous business ventures, all of which came to grief. They have a million and one sad tales of woe. Misfortune follows them everywhere. Inevitably, whenever I hire this type of individual, the same thing happens. They strike out in their new job as well.

Psychologists say that paradoxical behavior contrary to a person's true capabilities often indicates a game is being played. Players of this game would rather accept a small loss up-front if it eliminates the chance of losing big-time further down the line. For example, missing an appointment because a person loses track of time may be more acceptable and less threatening than the risk of botching the appointment itself. That way, the person can maintain the flattering illusion that success would have followed if it hadn't been for that pesky little failing of sometimes forgetting to show up on time for appointments.

Why is the specter of failure so debilitating to such people? Why are their paper-thin egos so easily shredded? Why do professional screw-ups persist in screwing up? Do underachievers feel unworthy? Deficient? Unlovable? Do they every once in a while have to go out and prove that their self-images are correct—that they are natural-born losers?

Psychologists have studied various factors contributing toward high self-esteem. A person's early family life seems to have the strongest influence. People who have high self-esteem tend to have had benevolent despots as parents—parents who succeeded in communicating to their children that they were significant people worthy of their abiding interest. These parents usually were strict and consistent in the enforcement of rules but weren't harsh; they were open to dissent and persuasion from the child.

We can't choose our parents, but we can adopt techniques later on to overcome poor self-esteem. These involve such things as self-analysis, self-persuasion, affirmations, and the creation of vivid positive mental pictures.

Creating new beliefs about oneself is, of course, a heck of a lot easier said than done. I am not qualified to help you change your self-image. But I do know that I encounter business people all of the time who experience recurring failures for no good reason at all. If your background has such a pattern to it, I suggest you seek professional help before trying again. In the business world, wimpy egos get gobbled up faster than computer-game images.

CHAPTER 10

MIND OVER MATTER

*If you are not fired with enthusiasm, then you will be fired
with enthusiasm.*   Vince Lombardi

Many people encounter something called *Weltschmerz* when they reach
middle age. *Weltschmerz* is the sentimental sadness that often occurs
when a person realizes that reality doesn't coincide with his or her expectations. Young people are not as easily afflicted by this feeling. There
is plenty of time left to excel when we are young. This leaves room for optimism. Being high on the vigor of youth, all we need is the patience to
wait for something good to happen.

Then—WHUMP!—middle age hits. The dust settles around our 40th
birthday. We rub our eyes and look around. Suddenly it hits home that
our options have shrunk and our opportunities have shriveled.
Aaaaaagh! Willy Loman lives! We are of modest means and meager
prospects. Off there in the distance goes the success bandwagon with all
the beautiful people aboard, celebrating on their way to Fun City and
Who's Who. Meanwhile, the rest of us are left behind, dutifully punching
time clocks. For most of us, life isn't fireworks and music. Rather, it is
filled with giant pillows. Occasionally, we strike out kicking and scream-
ing, but our fuss is muffled by anonymity and obscurity.

Many people are stricken with middle-age ennui these days, and it
often causes them to seek changes in their life-style, such as quitting
their jobs and going into business for themselves. They say things like,
"This job sucks," "Nobody appreciates me around here," "Time is passing me by," "I'm getting nowhere fast."

As a result, many people enter the small business world out of sheer boredom and frustration with their present situation. As employees, they feel stifled and unfulfilled. They sense they are mere nobodies sitting anonymously as stuffing for some giant corporation's furniture. For anyone who feels this way, there is tremendous appeal to jumping out and starting one's own business. The idea of being one's own boss is very attractive to a person whose waking hours are spent being a small cog in a giant machine. What downtrodden employee hasn't dreamed of shouting "take this job and shove it!" and marching out the door to start a successful Ganipganop franchise?

A word of caution: Before assuming the risk of starting your own business, by all means analyze your goals, evaluate your emotional state of mind, and assess your motives. If escapism is the driving force, fine. The fire may be no better than the frying pan, but at least it represents a change of scenery. But don't expect success in small business if this is the extent of your motives. Success in small business depends upon a "fire in the belly" rather than an "itch on the tummy." As far as your mental outlook is concerned, your business must be an end rather than a means. It must be "meat and drink and man and wife," a consuming passion that dominates your daily existence. Motivation, in other words, isn't just important; it is everything.

One of the coaches of my college rowing team, years ago, was a venerable old Englishman named George. George was a colorful philosopher oozing wisdom from every pore. Before a race, he used to say, "Boys, *yu've gaught ti waunt ti do it!*" My teammates and I never quite realized what old George was alluding to at the time, which may explain why we never won many crew races. However, George's words have sunk in deeper with every passing year. In order to accomplish something, in order to achieve a goal, you have to *want* to do it. You have to emotionalize your goals.

If you happen to be a member of the gifted one-in-a-million club, congratulations. For you, goods things fall into place without special effort. Otherwise, as a rule, your level of achievement will vary in direct proportion to your desires. This is true regardless of the mental, emotional, or physical baggage you carry.

If you go to bed at night dreaming of your goal, if it dominates your thoughts throughout the day, if you want it so badly you can taste and feel it, then sooner or later whatever potential you possess will be directed toward that end. When all of your brain waves are focused on your heart's desire, you maximize the chance for success. I cannot overemphasize this point: your best shot lies in achieving the mental state of bartering your very soul for the goal. But it must originate from a wellspring located deep within.

We perform much better when doing something we intrinsically enjoy, because internal motivation is a more powerful driving force than material rewards. When the fires of the psyche are stoked by strong internal desires, we are spurred to higher levels of accomplishment than external motivators such as money can generate. (For a discussion of factors involved in creating motivation within a business, see chapter three of *In Search of Excellence* by Thomas J. Peters and Robert H. Waterman.)

"Willing" your way to success may sound mystical, but, to a certain extent, it works. Perhaps that is why so many successful business people are of the "poor-kids-who-made-it-on-their-own" types. (For a description of the prevalence of poor or modest backgrounds in successful business people, see *Winning Performance: How America's High-Growth Midsize Companies Succeed* by Donald K. Clifford, Jr., and Richard E. Cavanagh.) Strong motivation overcomes an awful lot. Nearly all of us encounter people from time to time who emerge triumphant over great handicaps and personal disadvantages.

Some years ago, a wiry little French Canadian named Jacques became log-rolling champion of North America. Jacques's ability as a log roller was absolutely uncanny. His opponents would try every sort of strategy—rolling the log forward, rolling the log backwards, or jumping vigorously up and down on it. But, afterwards, there would be Jacques, perched like a wet parrot on the other end of the log.

A reporter once asked Jacques why no one seemed able to shake him off a log into the water. Jacques replied, "I no can fall off zee log."

The reporter said, "Yes, I know, but why is that so?"

Jacques replied, "I no can fall off zee log. I no can *sweem!*"

That, ladies and gentlemen, is motivation.

Belvedere   Maurits C. Escher

CHAPTER 11

SEEING BEYOND YOUR NOSE

Nothing is more likely to cause ruination in business than lack of perspective. Without a good sense of perspective, business management alternates between overreacting and underreacting. Lack of perspective causes people to respond to superficial stimuli rather than to underlying causes. It makes us jump at loud noises, yet allows us to race speeding freight trains to the crossing.

It causes tunnel vision and can't-see-the-forest-for-the-trees vision, both common afflictions in the business world. Professor C. Northcote Parkinson describes lack of perspective in his "Law of the Point of Vanishing Interest." Parkinson claims that corporate directors will argue endlessly over spending several thousand dollars on a new storage shed but will pass without comment appropriations that will cost millions of dollars. Several thousand they can relate to, but millions are beyond anyone's comprehension.

On a lesser scale, a small business person will argue like mad over a hundred-dollar increase in monthly rent but won't spend any time at all reevaluating the location of the business, a factor potentially worth thousands of dollars.

I continually encounter people who are intrigued with some small aspect of their business, which they proceed to beat to death, while they neglect more important affairs, until the situation erupts into a full-scale Mt. St. Helens. They will do things such as:

- Harass $12,000-a-year clerks in the front office but ignore production workers out in the plant who are earning $36,000 a year

- Spend copious hours fussing around in the shop doing a foreman's job instead of trying to generate more sales and new customers

- Exhaust themselves satisfying the whims of a few vocal, marginal customers, while neglecting important customers who are silent (silent, that is, until their feet speak as they move their business to a competitor)

- Be extremely cost-conscious regarding small office overhead items but lax in granting credit to new customers.

Many people carry on this way because they fear making decisions of major import. By immersing themselves in a quagmire of petty details, they avoid the trauma of having to make important decisions and major commitments that could drastically alter their lives. This sort of behavior, obviously, is evidence of a poor sense of perspective.

CPAs may seem to be an unimaginative bunch, but they do deserve credit for promoting an idea that has profound philosophical significance for business as a whole. It is the concept known as the materiality principle. According to this principle, professional auditors don't analyze accounts or make adjustments unless they have the potential to materially impact the overall picture. This approach may seem incongruous coming from nit-pickers and bean counters, but it is true. Professional auditing standards promulgated by CPAs revolve around materiality considerations. "Pass, immaterial," is their stock phrase. It is the philosophy of spending audit time doing what is truly important without getting tangled up in a web of small details, of evaluating matters as to whether they are material in relation to the total scheme of things.

You should run your business affairs the same way that CPAs audit a business' books. Life is too short and our days are too numbered to concentrate on petty cash. The materiality principle says: Focus on the big bucks instead. But you need perspective to implement the materiality principle. You must examine things with a telescope and a microscope as well as with your own eyes to make a materiality judgment.

So, how do you acquire perspective? Some lucky souls seem to be born with this attribute. In case you haven't been so endowed, here are a few tips:

The first rule is: Always procrastinate when considering a major problem. Sleep on it first. Allow some time to pass before making an important decision. A night's sleep works wonders on a person's point of view. What looks important today may seem trivial tomorrow or next week or next month. So, don't make a hasty decision when major issues are involved.

Second, take vacations. The typical small-business person becomes stuck to their business like a wet T-shirt and can't see beyond the confines of his or her own office. You should regularly get away from it all. Two weeks walled off from the phone in a completely different environment is guaranteed to clear your head. Monumental insights may be gained at the end of a fishing pole. In addition, take short breaks once in a while. Leave the shop and go to an afternoon movie or sit on a park bench. Temporarily remove yourself from the situation. Society's nose-to-the-grindstone work ethic may cause pangs of guilt the first few times you do this, but these feelings can be overcome if you persist. My favorite spot is a small park located on a hill overlooking town. When bullets are whizzing thick and fast around my head, I sometimes leave the office and sit there in my car for a half hour or so. These little interludes help me retrieve a sense of equilibrium. The principle to remember is this: Perspective grows in direct proportion to time and distance.

Third, find someone outside of your own business with whom you can talk openly. There is a huge world out there; staying in touch with it helps keep your own affairs in proper perspective. As the former coach of USC John McKay used to say, "One billion Chinese could care less whether or not USC wins the Rose Bowl." (Actually McKay did confess that he once received a letter from a disgruntled fan in China after USC lost a game to Notre Dame.) The point is, it is important to be able to kick things around with someone who is removed from your personal situation. Just hearing your own thoughts expressed out loud can be helpful. It may be your bartender, your CPA, your banker, or one of your Kiwanis buddies—just so he or she isn't emotionally involved with your personal problems.

Fourth, laugh. Laugh loud and laugh often. Humor releases tension. And it also helps create perspective. Learn to appreciate the ridiculousness of yourself and your situation. A person's sense of humor is probably the best indicator of his or her degree of sanity, and maintaining one's sanity is essential when running a small business.

Some laws of business parallel the laws of science. According to the uncertainty principle of physics, the smaller a particle is and the faster it is moving, the less sure we can be of its exact location. Similarly, the uncertainty principle of business says that the smaller the investment in a company and the fewer the number of people involved, the more uncertain we are of the company's profitability. As more people are added, the more their individual idiosyncrasies cancel out one another; and the more investment is fed into the business, the less risky the project becomes. As a consequence, uncertainty decreases to balance the equation.

That is why small business enterprises are such risky propositions. When the operation shrinks to one person, all that individual's screwball, nutty ideas have full reign. And if a modest investment is involved, all it takes is one adverse economic hiccup to blow the whole deal.

CHAPTER 12

GOALS ARE AN

ENTREPRENEUR'S BEST FRIEND

When a man does not know what harbor he is making for,
no wind is the right wind. Seneca

Closely related to the problem of developing perspective is the problem of working toward long-range goals. Most of us have enough foresight to pursue short-range goals because we tend to live for the moment. But striving toward long-range goals is a comparatively rare activity.

There are many, many details to be taken care of personally by the typical small business owner. With all of the distractions of a normal working day, keeping one's attention directed toward long-range goals is difficult. Consequently, most small business people plod along, one step at a time, staring at pebbles on the ground rather than looking for landmarks on the horizon. From a practical standpoint, the long-range overview of their daily activities is fourth-dimension stuff. Only in moments of great trauma, like when their lives are threatened, do they ever see their daily labors in true perspective.

Falling into this routine is easy, because we live our lives in small increments. Our attention usually lasts for only minutes at a time, sometimes for an hour, occasionally for as much as a whole day, and, on rare occasions, for a week or more. By implementing long-range goals, we can take advantage of this attribute because success is governed by the rules of integral calculus—the mathematics of the accumulation of many small increments. That is, most successes occur only after the accumulation of many small steps along the way. By focusing on long-range goals, we create small increments that are meaningful. Without long-range goals, our daily actions tend to be an aimless, random drift.

Goals are important not only for the direction they provide, but also for the incentive and motivation they generate. Goal striving is the essence of life itself. As the old Arab proverb goes, "The worst thing that can happen is to achieve everything you wanted out of life." The most mundane activity becomes interesting if there is a goal connected with it. Peeling potatoes, for example, is drudgery of drudgeries. But if you are trying to set a new world's record peeling potatoes suddenly it becomes an interesting science.

Big business is well aware of the practical benefits that can be harvested from a program of goal setting. Formal establishment of long-range goals is considered by big business to be an essential management tool. It is called *strategic planning*. Small business people, on the other hand, tend to regard the process as an abstract concept. This is unfortunate, because goal setting is a powerful technique.

The act of setting goals, however, needs to be a conscious, premeditated activity. It is something you must sit down and force yourself to do. Unfortunately, most small business people become so harried and distracted during the course of a day they don't think of such things. Or, if they do, it is in terms too vague to be effective. From a practical standpoint, three factors need to exist before a long-range goal becomes an effective motivator:

1. It has to be something you want very, very badly, and it must have strong emotional and psychological appeal.

2. You have to be capable of vividly imagining the results if actually attained. In other words, it has to be something specific and concrete rather than sketchy or hazy.

3. You have to believe sincerely that it is attainable. Pie-in-the-sky goals are not going to be pursued with much enthusiasm. For example, you might be thrilled to death to date a Hollywood sex symbol, and you might be able to vividly imagine what it would be like. But you know this is as likely to happen as your

having tea with the Queen of England. So, as a goal, the idea is worthless.

The important thing to remember, though, is that establishing goals has to be done consciously and willfully. Discipline yourself to periodically think about your goals. Make it a thinking habit. It is best to analyze goals in writing. Expressing them on paper makes the process less abstract. Likewise, putting your thoughts in writing helps expose conflicts and establish priorities. For example, which goal comes first—opening up a branch operation next year, or cutting debts and interest expense?

Also, keep in mind it isn't *setting* goals that's important. It's *having* goals that counts. There is a subtle, but vital, difference. Verbalizing a goal is not the same as internalizing and assimilating it into your psyche. Having it permeate your very being is what creates a sense of direction. Memorializing a goal on paper helps reinforce this process. Then periodically review and revise your written list of goals. You may feel silly doing this sort of thing. But, take my word for it, it works.

Finally, keep in mind that goals must be specific. Broad abstractions don't cut it, because they are too intangible. A goal must be something you can relate to in terms of precise action and activities. For example, making a net profit of $100,000 next year is not a goal. It is a result. Many things contribute toward boosting your net profit, such as increased sales, higher profit margins, lower overhead, different work habits, change in product lines, more effective promotion, upgrading equipment, moving to a new location, and so on. So where do you begin?

On the other hand, selling 100,000 widgets next year in the city of St. Louis is a goal. It is something you can sink your teeth into. Cutting overhead salaries by 20 percent is also a goal. It is something you probably can translate into specific overt action. So go get that goal, tiger!

Never look back. Something may be gaining on you.   Gary Larson

CHAPTER 13

THE HASSLE FACTOR CURVE

One of the biggest puzzlements I've seen observing the antics of small business people is how many dumb things are done by otherwise smart people. People who, in most other respects, are intelligent, well balanced, and sane. Why is this so? Why are so many small business feet riddled with self-inflicted gunshot wounds? I'm convinced it's because most people really don't want to make money—big money, that is—because if they did, they would. How can that be? How can anyone not want to make money? Because many people intuitively recognize that achieving greater financial rewards would involve actions contrary to their basic nature—things they can't imagine themselves doing, the thought of which invokes deep-seated anxiety.

What I've just described is a manifestation of the hassle factor curve phenomenon. This is the final character trait of successful small business people I'm going to mention. In the last analysis, it may be the most critical of all. This phenomenon stems from the tendency toward a direct relationship between money and stress. That is, the further one progresses economically, the more one encounters a stress-generating environment. The competitive forces driving the capitalistic system dictate this to be so.

By and large, the easiest jobs to perform in our society are the ones that offer the least financial rewards. For example, being a janitor is an honorable and honest profession, but many people qualify for that job's requirements. Being a successful operator of a complex, diversified business, on the other hand, requires skills not commonly possessed—mental, emotional, psychic, and otherwise.

Clinging with one hand to the rungs of a swaying economic ladder while swatting away competitors with the other, people at the top lead lives that are anything but tranquil. The responsibilities and uncertainties connected with earning a place in the sun make for continuing episodes of stress. In fact, we can count on an increased level of stress, the more we struggle for incremental increases in income.

Obviously, this is a general statement, and exceptions do occur. In a society as complex and dynamic as ours, it sometimes happens that high incomes are achieved with very little stress. Some people do win lotteries. For most people, though, the general rule prevails. Wealth does not accumulate without encountering stressful problems along the way.

It is also true that human nature abhors stress, particularly protracted stress. As we go through life, caroming from titillation to trepidation to tribulation, we desperately seek the confines of our comfort zones. Oh sure, we strive to make money and get ahead, but our strivings are held in check by psychological hang-ups and emotional limitations. Our activities are drawn like magnetized particles to our personal comfort zones. We act like the person who searches for a lost wallet on the opposite side of the street because that is where the street lamp is located.

There's a Faustian aspect to being an entrepreneur. The more one seeks money and economic power, the more one's soul is sold to the "stress devil." The further one's psyche falls into "stress hell," the more one wants to escape.

Few folks are obsessed to the same degree as Faust, who sold his whole inventory of soul. Of course, Faust was pursuing love as well as material wealth. Most people gravitate toward equilibrium, a balance between money and stress. According to the hassle factor curve theory, the more money people earn, the less incremental stress they are willing to accept. This principle is illustrated in the graph below.

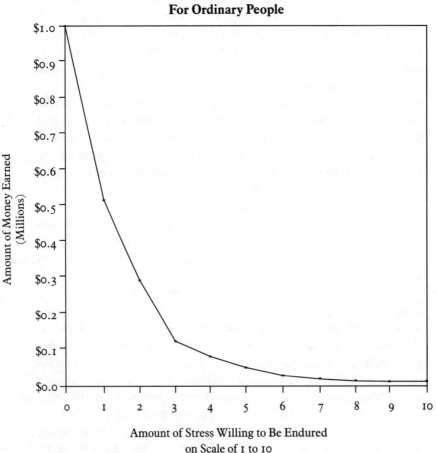

Hassle Factor Curve
For Ordinary People

Amount of Stress Willing to Be Endured
on Scale of 1 to 10

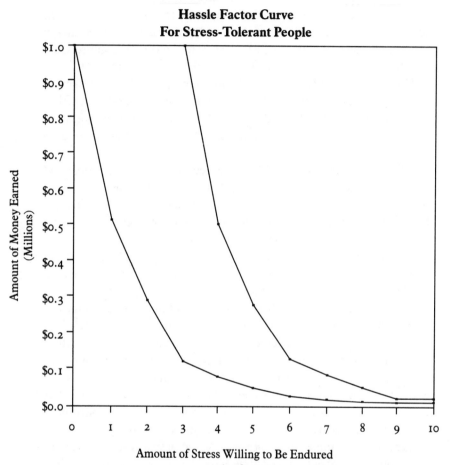

Hassle Factor Curve
For Stress-Tolerant People

Amount of Money Earned (Millions)

Amount of Stress Willing to Be Endured
on scale of 1 to 10

    The hassle factor curve theory is universally applicable. It predicts that people will endure enormous stress to earn the bare-bones minimum for survival. However, as they earn progressively more, they are less willing to endure stress. Most humans will do practically anything to avoid starvation. But when their bellies are full, these same individuals will cut back on the amount of hassles they will tolerate.

    Give them a TV, a VCR, and a car, and they will put up with even less.

After they earn their first million, why knock themselves out for another million? If it is there for the taking, sure, no one is about to turn down easy pickings. But the amount of emotional, physical, and mental energy they are willing to invest to acquire an extra million or two is appreciably less than what they were willing to endure to make their first pile.

This principle holds true for people in general, but there is one feature that is vital to understand. Individual hassle factor curves do not utilize the same horizontal and vertical scales. After all, stress is relative: what is inordinately stressful to one individual may only be mildly stressful to another.

This is often an essential difference between successful people and those not so successful. The successful ones can endure more stress per dollar. They can tolerate situations that would cause an average person to hide under the bed. As a consequence, the hassle factor curve of a stress-tolerant person is different from that of an "ordinary" person.

Low stress tolerance is the prime reason many people don't attain their avowed goals. Consequently, a soul-searching evaluation of your hassle factor curve is a must if economic success is truly what you seek.

Okay, you've given yourself a stress check and conclude you come un-glued when the stress monster appears. When stress says "Boo!" a panic-flight reaction is triggered. You have two choices: you can either limit your activities to those that stay within the boundaries of your com-fort zone, or you can try to master your feelings and stretch your bound-aries. The latter choice offers an opportunity for self-advancement, but it is not an easy path to follow. As far as human nature is concerned, avoiding stress is natural, whereas seeking stress is unnatural.

Hence, the dilemma: How does one succeed in small business without developing permanently frazzled nerves? How do you avoid a terminal case of the work-yourself-into-a-tizzy syndrome? You must find ways to live with the hassles. A number of techniques have been developed that enable a person to better deal with tension and stress. They range all the way from such things as physical exercise and creative hobbies to con-scious relaxation techniques, meditation, and cultivation of positive at-titudes. It is beyond the scope of this book to delve into the subject. But if you feel the need to improve how you handle stress, it might be wise to seek out a stress management class where these sorts of techniques are taught. There are also a number of good books on the subject. I recommend *Stress Management* by Edward Charlesworth and Ronald Nathan.

There are two different aspects, though, to stress tolerance. Being able to endure stress physically and emotionally is one thing. Being able to function intelligently and effectively under stress is quite another. I'll give you an example of the latter.

Two Canadian trappers were coming home from checking their trap lines. As they trudged along the barren tundra, off on the horizon, they saw an object.

"I wonder if that could be some kind of animal?" asked one of the trappers.

As they walked further, the object grew larger.

"You know, I wonder if that could be a bear," said the other trapper. A few minutes later, it became obvious that the object was, indeed, a bear. Furthermore, it was a big, mean-looking grizzly bear, and it was coming straight toward them. The two trappers stopped and pondered their plight. They were out of ammunition, and there were no trees nearby to climb. One of the trappers took off his pack, rummaged around, and pulled out a pair of tennis shoes. Then he sat down, removed his boots, and started to put on the tennis shoes. The other trapper looked down at him incredulously.

"What do you think you are doing, Pierre?" he asked. "You know perfectly well a man can't outrun a bear."

Pierre didn't even bother to look up. He just kept lacing his tennis shoes.

"Who said anything about trying to outrun the bear?" he said. "I figure all I have to do is outrun you!"

CHAPTER 14

A CASE STUDY

Enough abstractions. How about a live example to illustrate what I've been talking about? Here is a true story about a successful entrepreneur named Julie. To appreciate Julie's accomplishments, it will help if you imagine yourself in her shoes. I will remind you to step into them at crucial points throughout the narration.

Julie and Harold are married, have one child, and are in their thirties. Harold has a degree in electrical engineering. Julie used to be a high school teacher. Today, she owns a small company that designs and manufactures ceramic jewelry. Harold works for Julie as the company's marketing manager.

Julie's company has nearly 30 employees and sells primarily to stores and boutiques on the West Coast, although some sales are now being made in the East as well. The company operates in the black and is growing. Its product line is upper-end fashion. Here is how Julie's business came into being.

Julie taught art classes in high school while putting Harold through college. Things were a bit tight, but they were squeaking by and eagerly anticipating the day when Harold would graduate and become gainfully employed.

It came to pass that Julie's high school encountered budget problems. Julie was unexpectedly called upon to teach ceramics in addition to her regular art classes. The only problem was she knew nothing about ceramics. The furnaces and other lab equipment were a complete mystery to her.

This meant entering a self-taught cram course. By studying nights and weekends and experimenting in the ceramics lab, she was able to acquire enough knowledge to get by.

To increase her proficiency, Julie started designing and producing ceramic earrings for practice, which she occasionally wore to class. Students noticed and admired Julie's creations. They asked her to make them copies as well. Julie was flattered and happily obliged. Her earrings quickly became the rage.

One evening, while contemplating the depressed state of their finances, she had an intriguing thought: "Since my ceramic earrings are so popular, why give them away? Why not make a little money by selling them?"

(Okay, suppose this had been you. Would you have had the initiative to actually do something about it? Or would you have let the thought remain in your idle daydream bag?)

Julie took action. She approached the school administrators. "Would it be all right," she asked, "if I used school facilities on occasion to produce ceramic products for myself?" She was given an okay as long as it was after school hours and on her own time.

Julie went to work designing and producing earrings and other jewelry items in the school ceramics lab at night. Then she commenced traipsing around the countryside on weekends trying to sell her creations to boutiques and small shops. The ensuing months were an education as well as a tribulation. Doors slammed in her face and criticisms were frequent. Sometimes she made a few sales and on occasion she heard a few complimentary words of encouragement. Overall, though, it was discouraging, and sometimes she would arrive home in tears.

(The first big moment of truth. Would you have stuck it out any further? Or would you have crumpled under all of the put-downs?)

Julie didn't crumple. Gradually her skin grew thicker and she slowly acquired selling skills as well as insights as to what items had greater sales appeal. After a year of much effort and modest sales, it became apparent that selling "onesies" and "twosies" to small shops had limited potential. She needed large volume sales to big outlets.

(If you were Julie, what action would you have taken to seek bigger markets? Or would you merely have complained "woe is me" to your friends?)

Julie didn't moan and groan. She gathered her courage and sought an audience with the head buyer of one of the country's most fashionable and successful department store chains. Wham! Another door in the face. Julie discovered that buyers for prestigious stores are as hard to get to as the president of the United States.

(How many people would have put their tail between their legs and skulked off at this point? How would you have reacted?)

Julie was persistent and resourceful. She hung around until she uncovered the name of the person having authority to approve her product. Then she turned herself into a pest. It took a whole year, but eventually Julie was granted an appointment with Ms. Big Cheese Buyer.

Julie displayed her wares, gave her pitch, and waited with thumping heart for the buyer to speak: "You know, this just might have some potential for us. Tell you what, we'll let you have a trunk sale."

At a trunk sale, a supplier is given access to store facilities to set up a temporary sales display, just like a vendor out on the street. The supplier's future relationship with the store depends on how much he or she sells from the display. Julie's trunk sale was successful enough to convince the buyer to order some of Julie's jewelry creations.

After a while, Julie and the buyer came to be on cordial terms. One day the buyer took Julie aside and said, "Look, kid, if you are going to do much business with us, here is what I am going to have to see from you." Then she described product styles and concepts that Julie would have to come up with to be a hit at the jewelry counter.

(How many people would have procrastinated before responding to this sort of advice? How quickly would you have reacted?)

Julie dug right in, working night and day for several weeks designing and creating a new product line. The buyer was pleased and placed a big order. Having such a prestigious customer gave Julie's company status and created entries into other major stores. Sales took off. Employees were hired and sales reps were retained. Harold finally graduated, but instead of seeking a job in electrical engineering, he went to work for Julie.

The market for fashion jewelry is fickle and competitive. The company works hard to stay in the forefront of fashion and style and continually experiments with new techniques and new products. But Julie's company is well established and must now be considered a bona fide success.

Now then, how does the foregoing vignette square with the things we've talked about? It correlates very closely.

Did Julie exhibit people skills? Of course she did. Julie constantly had to deal with people on the way up and had to enlist their assistance as well as their patronage. Her personality greased the skids.

Was aggression involved? You bet. It took gutsy, hard-nosed fortitude to persevere in the face of put-downs and run-arounds.

Did Julie demonstrate adroitness in sizing up people? Certainly. Julie displayed an astute sense of which way the wind was blowing when it came to dealing with people.

Did Julie have a healthy ego and self-esteem? How else could she have survived the rejections and disappointments? How could she have found the chutzpa to go after a high-level, mucky-muck buyer?

Did Julie show a driving motivation? No one could have accomplished what she did without being highly motivated. At several points along the line, most people would have said, "Screw it. Who needs this?"

How about a sense of perspective? Absolutely. Julie proved very adept at figuring out what was really important.

Did Julie engage in long-range goal setting? Without a doubt. That's how she kept herself pointed in the right direction.

Did she demonstrate a high level of stress tolerance? I'll say. Despite difficulties and hassles, Julie kept her spirits up and didn't wimp out by succumbing to disappointments.

That's what it takes, kids. It ain't easy, but it's certainly possible. The Julies of this world prove it to be so.

PART THREE

PRACTICAL SUGGESTIONS

FOUND IN THE REALM OF

THE NITTY AND THE GRITTY

In the animal self-help section   Gary Larson

CHAPTER 15

THE "HOW TO" CHAPTER

Many bookstores have a self-improvement section in which they display that special category known as how-to books. These are the happy-faced, upbeat treatises that tell readers how to solve personal problems or how to do something. If you've spent any time in bookstores, you know the genre. The phrase *how to* normally pops up in the title. Some examples are *How to Get Rich, How to Marry the Man of Your Choice, How to Pick Up Girls, How to Master the Art of Selling, How to Start Your Own Business and Succeed,* and *How to Avoid Stress.* In other words, "How to Do This, That, and Everything."

The how-to delivery exists in TV and seminar format as well. Late-night cable TV hucksters blat out their beguiling enticements: "how to become the new *you* you've always wanted to be . . . how to achieve financial success . . . how to find the mate of your choice . . . how to relieve stress . . . how to lose weight without effort . . . how to repattern your life practically overnight . . . just go to the phone and order right now!"

Is there anyone who hasn't felt inadequate or frustrated at times regarding some aspect of his or her life? Breathes there a man so dead who hasn't cursed the gods for his afflictions? Of course not. How-to books promise simple answers to common problems. They claim practical, easy-to-implement solutions. That is why their appeal is so powerful and why publishers love them. Who doesn't yearn for a magic wand? With splashy promotion and the hook of an enticing how-to title, such books lure many a hopeful customer to the cash register. I certainly have bought my share over the years.

But how-to programs usually serve up cotton candy rather than real food. Simple answers to complex problems are invariably too limited in scope to be effective. And easy solutions to deep-seated difficulties are nearly always ineffectual. As cynic Edward Dolmick once remarked, "In real life, you don't get rich quick, flatten your stomach in five minutes a day, or learn French while you sleep."

Forget about the how-to approach here. I'm not claiming magic solutions. Just school-of-hard-knocks insights. At the same time, I'm not saying a person can't change. Of course you can. But let's be realistic. Any changes that you undergo will normally occur over an extended period of time and will be confined to the basic framework of your personality. Yes, you can change and, yes, you can improve, but it will be a long project that will be restricted to your innate talents and capabilities. Therefore, if you are serious about self-improvement, concentrate your efforts on seeking ways to commit yourself to a sustained effort rather than searching for a quick fix.

There are some things you can do that will help give you the endurance to achieve self-improvement goals. So this is my how-to section. Basically, I would like to put a few killer bees in your bonnet. Read on. (What's that strange buzzing in my head?)

Up to this point, considerable analysis and discussion have been thrown at you. The personal qualities required for success in small business have been described. By now, you might be saying, "That's all well and good, but how do I develop those qualities?" Here are some suggestions.

First of all, fall back upon the wisdom of the ages. Two thousand years ago, Aristotle said, "Know thyself." Modern psychologists still can't top that approach. The first thing to do is assess your qualities and characteristics. In other words, know thyself. (Remember my previous harpings on the importance of tuning in to reality?) Know your strengths, weaknesses, proclivities, and motivations, and you will know your problems and potentialities. So, evaluate how you stack up with regard to the essential traits we've discussed previously. Here is a checklist to help you:

Self-Assessment Inventory

Trait	Very Strong	Pretty Good	Average	Poor
1. Personality (people skills)	___	___	___	___
2. Aggression (alphaness)	___	___	___	___
3. People radar (intuition)	___	___	___	___
4. Ego (self-esteem)	___	___	___	___
5. Motivation (fire in the belly)	___	___	___	___
6. Perspective (forest vs. trees)	___	___	___	___
7. Goal setting (long-range planning)	___	___	___	___
8. Stress tolerance (hassle factor)	___	___	___	___

It might be worthwhile to seek a second opinion for your self-assessment. Sometimes we aren't particularly realistic when we view ourselves. As that old proverb goes, "Others' faults are before our eyes; ours are behind us."

Assuming you can evaluate your traits reasonably accurately, post your self-assessment inventory where you will see it on a regular basis. The idea is to keep the evaluation and your reasons for preparing it in mind as you go about your daily life. Next, try to answer the following questions on a regular basis:

1. How can I emphasize and capitalize on my strong points?

2. How can I compensate for my weak points and work around them?

3. How can I improve on all points?

Granted, making yourself over in any substantial sense may be unrealistic. But don't try to tell me some improvement isn't possible. People do grow and mature. Just knowing what you need to improve upon is a big step forward. Creating a self-assessment inventory helps. Being continually aware of areas you need to work on will result in some improvement, assuming you have the will and motivation to do so.

Human potential seminars advocate frequent follow-ups to their courses. That's because people lose their enthusiasm and commitment once they leave the camp meeting environment of the seminar. Converting academic knowledge and intellectual insights into overt action is a quantum leap. That is why seminar attendees fall off the wagon and backslide into previous behavior patterns when they re-enter their own environment. The same thing happens when people engage in any kind of self-help activity.

So, it is important to keep self-improvement goals continually in focus. Otherwise, you have no chance of making them stick. The trick is to saturate your subconscious mind with them. Fortunately, the subconscious mind keeps functioning even when the rest of "us" is out to lunch. We can capitalize on this attribute by reinforcing self-improvement goals through verbalization until the goals are assimilated into the subconscious.

For example, say the following phrase 100 times: "I am a capable person who can deal with problems." Louder! Very good. Next, say 100 times: "I am a worthwhile human being who deserves success." With conviction! Good. This corny routine is known in the trade as using affirmations. It can be surprisingly effective if continued over a period of time. I know someone who leaves yellow self-stick notes all over his house as affirmation reminders of the things he is seeking to improve upon. He puts notes on the refrigerator door, the bathroom mirror, his dresser—even his car dashboard.

Another popular self-improvement technique is visualization. Sports psychologists are big on this one. The idea is to daydream. To visualize and imagine as vividly as possible successfully carrying out whatever it is you wish to accomplish, be it hitting a home run or making a dynamite sale.

These techniques work because the subconscious mind tends to confuse fantasy with fact. According to psychologists, the subconscious is embarrassingly gullible. By using affirmations and by visualizing success, the subconscious can, in effect, be conned into thinking that the attached person really is effective. Once this is achieved, it becomes a booster rocket to support conscious efforts. With the subconscious mind rooting for us, whispering in our ears, "You can do it!" the chances for accomplishment are much improved.

Equally important is figuring out how to play the cards that mother nature's gene-mixing system dealt us. One neat thing about being in business for yourself is that you are the boss. As such, you create the work assignments. This means being able to spend time in areas where you are most effective while letting employees do the rest. This allows you to work around personal weaknesses and concentrate instead on where your strengths lie.

For example, I have weak people radar. I tend to take people at face value and have difficulty recognizing duplicity. I am a sucker for con artists and snow jobs, and it shows. Car salesmen make soft cooing noises whenever I enter their lots. People have fooled me so often for so long I don't even try to figure them out anymore. That's why I delegate to my partners the task of interviewing prospective employees. Likewise, that's why I pawn off meetings involving negotiations. On the other hand, my analytical skills are strong, so my partners shove tax-planning problems and financial analyses my way. It's a matter of doing what you do best and avoiding tasks that take you past your level of competency.

Every normal person yearns to be more effective in his or her life, and trying to become more effective is not an unreasonable goal. But it is highly unlikely this will come about by some sort of overnight conversion. However, if you adhere to the simple techniques outlined above, someday you may wake up and discover that you have shed your cocoon and that the person you are today is far different from what you were when you started out.

CHAPTER 16

PANHANDLER WISDOM

We all agree that your theory is crazy. The question which divides us is whether it is crazy enough.   Niels Bohr, physicist (commenting on fellow physicist Wolfgang Pauli's new theory)

The most essential element in running a small business these days is keeping it simple. Complexities of the modern world boggle the mind and it gets worse every day. Today's small business person must have up-to-date working knowledge of such complicated subjects as finance; commercial law; income tax law; accounting; insurance; truth-in-lending laws; zoning ordinances; rights of minorities; the Disabled Americans Act; labor laws; federal, state, and local government regulations; environmental laws; union rules; immigration laws; technological developments; federal health and safety laws; and a thousand and one little details peculiar to his or her own trade or business. We are talking serious brain gridlock here, folks. Therefore, the less complicated a small business person's internal affairs, the better chance he or she has of coping.

The route to my office takes me every day through one of the raunchiest parts of the city. At times, this particular neighborhood is a veritable obstacle course of panhandlers. Every day I run the gantlet. The routine is always pretty much the same. As I walk down the street, some panhandler half a block away spots me coming toward him. Even from that distance, you can see his eyes light up as he perceives another customer entering his territory.

He wobbles around a bit, trying to focus so he can zero in. When I come within range, he straightens up, partially blocks my path and barks out a sharp "Hey!"—trying to break through my attempts to ignore him. He follows up with a hastily mumbled pitch for money. Unless he talks fast, though, he doesn't get a chance to finish because I always step up the pace and whisk on by—half loathing but also half frightened by the unpredictability of a person whose behavior is so foreign to my own.

Actually, it is surprising how effective modern-day panhandlers can be. If you watch one going through his routine from a distance, you'll see many a passerby fork over a few coins, hoping by this ransom to save the discomfort of prolonged personal contact.

This might seem a bizarre thought, but panhandlers make an ideal model for small business people to copy. To begin with, a panhandler's "product" is simple and has universal appeal. The prosperous never like being personally involved with squalor, nor do they like being reminded of its existence. For a small fee, the panhandler relieves his clients of the responsibility of viewing and interacting with a bit of life's unpleasantness—the panhandler himself.

He guarantees instant satisfaction. Give him a quarter and relief is only moments away. He has no problem with bad debts or slow receivables, because he deals strictly in cash. He has no overhead expense, no rent or salaries to pay, no utility bills, no capital outlay, no insurance payments, no company cars to keep up, and no trade unions to contend with.

Panhandlers never run out of customers; the streets are filled with prospects. They are in little danger from cheap foreign competition. They don't worry about technological obsolescence; no robot is ever going to be invented to replace them. And talk about tax shelters! Gifts are not taxable to the recipient, so panhandlers don't pay income tax. Nor do they pay property tax, luxury tax, inventory tax, business and occupational tax, self-employment tax, payroll tax, or excise tax. Finally, panhandling is an activity that, by its very nature, does not lend itself to exploitation by big business. And it is not something that can easily be franchised.

Portraying panhandlers as a business model might seem weird, but the simplicity of their economic activity is something all small business people should strive for.

CHAPTER 17

THE WAGES OF UNREASONABLENESS
ARE PROFITS

"What has he ever done?" the lady inquired. . . . "Well,
up in the Lehigh Valley once he talked a mocking bird out
of a tree." A. J. Liebling

One aspect of being in business for yourself is hard to accept: It is often advantageous to be unreasonable. The reason for this is simple.

Small business owners are perpetually in an adversarial position. They must hassle with employees, revenue agents, suppliers, customers, banks, governmental agencies, and, of course, competitors. Most such squabbles involve give and take. That is, each side usually grants a few concessions to arrive at a settlement. Rarely are business disputes zero-sum games in which a clear winner and a clear loser are declared. Negotiation is the normal order of the day.

You, the small business person, will be seeking lower wages, lower taxes, lower purchase prices, higher sales prices, better bank terms, less government interference, and so forth. Those on the other side of the fence want the opposite.

In other words, very often you are in the position of having to argue. Arguing can develop into a fine art, if you let it. The classic format for arguing involves constructing paths of logic by applying two different types of formal reasoning—inductive and deductive. But the skills of a logician aren't necessary in everyday life. From a practical standpoint, you can get by if you remember that arguments between rational people are based either upon disagreements over facts or upon what principles apply. (For an excellent book on the subject of practical techniques for arguing, see *How to Win Arguments* by William A. Rusher.)

Most often, a reasonable argument revolves around participants trying to determine the facts and resolving what principles govern. For example:

Fact 1: The roof of your rented warehouse-office building leaks.

Fact 2: You did nothing to cause the leak.

Principle 1: The landlord pays for major repairs.

As a reasonable person, you present these points to your landlord. The landlord, on the other hand, argues that fact 2 is wrong because you caused the leak by storing materials on the warehouse roof. Also, that additional principles apply—that your lease specifically bans storage of materials on the roof and that tenants are responsible for any damages they cause.

But we are not talking reason here. As a matter of fact, we want to be unreasonable, appearing all the while, of course, to be scrupulously reasonable. So, remember the old lawyer's saying:

If the facts are against you, argue the law.
If the law is against you, argue the facts.
If both facts and law are against you, argue justice!

Continuing with the foregoing example, you now argue that the leak wasn't caused by storing materials on the roof (a fact?). Even if it had been, the roof should have been strong enough to support the materials without springing a leak (justice?). Roof leaks are an extraordinary repair, not an ordinary maintenance item (the law?). Your rent is too high (an opinionated fact?). You were thinking of renting more space from him but not if he is going to treat you this way (a questionable fact?). There are rats in the basement and cockroaches in the coffee lounge (an irrelevant fact?); the plumbing and electrical systems are substandard (an exaggerated fact?); your brother-in-law works for the building department (a threatening fact?); you have friends in high places (a vague threatening fact?). Finally, you argue that it just isn't fair, because, after all, you have always been a good tenant and, besides, it is his building, not yours (justice?).

Get the idea? Here's another example, this one from the world of whimsy. The comic strip "Bloom County" once had a delightful episode depicting a debate between two of its characters. The dialogue went like this:

> *Milo:* I understand that my opponent supports the 55 mph speed limit.
> *Opus:* Saves 50,000 lives a year. I fully support saving lives.
> *Milo:* Then he'd support the saving of another 10,000 lives by lowering the limit to 40 mph.
> *Opus:* 40?
> *Milo:* Or to 20. . . . Saving 30,000 lives a year.
> *Opus:* Gee, 20 is pretty slow.
> *Milo:* Apparently my opponent would send 30,000 men, women, and children to fiery, mangled deaths just so he can zoom along to his manicurist at 55.
> *Opus:* I don't have a manicurist!
> *Milo:* He probably doesn't. Most mass murderers don't. Hitler didn't.

At this point, Opus becomes so flummoxed and discombobulated that he dissolves into a blithering idiot.

What are the fallacies in Milo's argument and why did Opus fail to exploit them? One fallacy is assuming that the principle of saving human lives takes precedence over all other principles. Actually, heartless as it may sound, other principles sometimes supercede. One, of course, is maintaining a healthy economy and a viable infrastructure. Dropping the speed limit to 20 mph undoubtedly would reduce traffic deaths but, at the same time, would hamstring commerce and create enormous inconvenience to society as a whole.

Another fallacy is assuming that car crashes are the only cause of death impacted by a 20 mph speed limit. The devastated economy resulting from such a change would likely cause many indirect deaths from poverty and malnutrition.

Opus's first mistake was to let himself be hypnotized into focusing on only one principle when others also apply. His second mistake was to let Milo concentrate on one fact (a low speed limit will result in fewer traffic deaths) when another overriding fact existed (a low speed limit will cause great discomfort and inconvenience from a ruined economy).

Opus's final mistake was to let himself be distracted by Milo's cheap debating trick of using emotionally weighted words and name calling—e.g., "fiery," "mangled deaths," "mass murderers," and "Hitler" (called *argumentums ad populum* and *ad hominem* in the debating trade). By defending himself against baseless accusations and insinuations, Opus forgot the main argument.

Debate tactics are useful to know, but business disputes aren't structured as formally. From a practical standpoint, when two individuals negotiate from opposite points of view, they usually arrive at a middle-ground compromise. For example, Smith and Jones have gotten into a rip-roaring argument over Smith's bill for emergency repairs to Jones's waste storage tank. Smith's position is at point "A" in the diagram below. He says he is due $2,000 for the repair work. Jones's position is at point "B" in the diagram. He claims Smith's bill is excessive and shouldn't exceed $1,000. Assume their positions are reasonable from each individual's point of view.

After taking their respective stances, Smith and Jones will negotiate and bargain until each determines where the other's hard-core position lies. Once this has been determined, they will jockey around for a compromise. Their compromise may fall close to "A" or it may fall close to "B." However, based upon normal probability frequency distribution curves, it most likely will land near the middle—$1,500. That is why

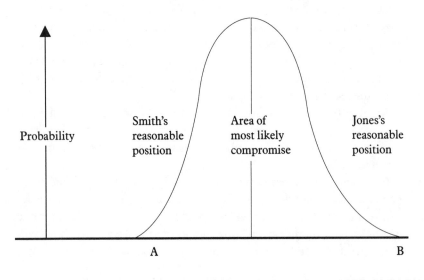

Probability | Smith's reasonable position | Area of most likely compromise | Jones's reasonable position

A   B

judges often decide court cases on the basis of a 50-50 split between plaintiff and defendant.

The foregoing mechanism operates in practically all potential compromise situations and shows why unreasonableness can often be of benefit. Suppose that Smith, instead of taking a reasonable position at point "A," takes an unreasonable position at point "X": he hitches up his overalls and submits a bill for $3,000! Smith claims lots of overtime was involved, it was difficult to obtain parts, his other jobs had to be rescheduled, Jones's employees interfered with his work, EPA had to be consulted for pollution problems, and so forth. If Smith argues his unreasonable point "X" as convincingly as his reasonable point "A," he stretches the compromise probability curve his way, as shown in the diagram below. By assuming an unreasonable posture, Smith increases his chances of a more favorable compromise.

In actual negotiating situations, Smith's compromise may still end up closer to Jones's "B" than Smith's "A," but, by taking an unreasonable stance, Smith brings the probabilities more in his favor. The ultimate settlement will undoubtedly be closer to "A" than "B." Such are the facts of life in the art of negotiation.

However, to make unreasonableness work for you, you must be sure of one thing: your opponent must not know that you know your position is unreasonable. When taking an unreasonable position, you know you are

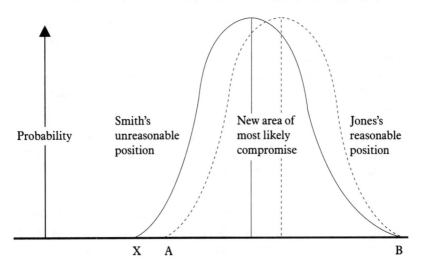

Probability

Smith's unreasonable position

New area of most likely compromise

Jones's reasonable position

X   A   B

being unreasonable and chances are your opponent knows you are being unreasonable. But if your opponent knows that *you* know you are being unreasonable, all is lost. Your opponent will simply ignore your unreasonable point "X" position and consider you to be standing at point "A" instead. Not only will your unreasonableness fail to stretch the compromise distribution curve, you will ruin your future unreasonableness credibility as well.

So, to make unreasonableness work, you must be good at the bluff. You must be a good actor. For most people, this takes practice. (For a good reference book on the techniques of negotiating, see *The Art of Negotiating* by Gerard I. Nierenberg.) My experiences as a CPA have exposed me to many unreasonable people. After years of personal observations, I have developed some tips to help you become a more successful unreasonable person.

Be congenial, courteous, and nice. If you behave obnoxiously or in an antagonistic manner, you risk arousing the emotions of your opponent to the point that he or she will refuse to respond reasonably to your unreasonableness and may even precipitate withdrawal from further negotiations. By being a "nice," albeit unreasonable person, you keep your opponent on the defensive. If your opponent throws a snit because of your unreasonableness, he or she will feel guilty, because nobody feels comfortable getting mad at a "nice" person.

Don't let your body language give you away. Maintain an earnest facial expression, avoid nervous twitches, adopt a self-righteous demeanor, and keep calm. It is absolutely essential you not give your opponent any hint that you know you are being unreasonable. If physical mannerisms indicate you realize you are on shaky ground, your opponent will immediately suspect the truth—that you are only bluffing.

Concede small issues at the beginning so as to appear reasonable. This again puts your opponent on the defensive. It also creates the impression you are trying to be reasonable and are endeavoring to reach a compromise.

Don't concede any of your opponent's points, however, without a fight. The objective is to wear down your opponent. Make him or her work for every small concession as though it were a major issue at stake.

The more emotionally worn out your opponent becomes, the more concessions you are likely to obtain.

Create false issues. Try to keep your opponent off the main issues about which you are being unreasonable. By putting forth baseless accusations and assertions, you will draw your opponent's fire and cause your opponent to "tilt with windmills." This saps his or her emotional energy and makes it appear you are being reasonable when you concede, after much arguing, that you were wrong on those points.

Avoid specifics. Try to generalize as much as possible, because generalizations are harder to deal with than specifics. Notice in the Smith-Jones argument that Smith used nonspecific statements as to why his bill was so high: lots of overtime was involved, it was difficult to obtain parts, there was interference by Jones's employees, EPA had to be consulted. How do you refute sweeping statements like those?

Don't lie about specifics. The problem with specific facts is they are too easy to check out. If you lie about them and are caught, it puts you on the defensive and discredits your whole unreasonable stance. If you are scrupulously truthful about specific facts, it lends credence to all the unreasonable things you say.

Allow your opponent room to save face! This is very important. In modern-day terms, this is called a win-win situation. Obtaining concessions from people is much easier if they think they are receiving concessions from you. Therefore, avoid issuing ultimatums and emphasize the concessions given the other side, regardless of how trivial or hollow they may be. Most people resist vigorously when they think they are being hung with the loss side of a win-lose situation. If they perceive this to be happening, they may opt for lose-lose, even if it means a larger loss for themselves.

A classic example is the time NFL football players went out on strike. Both the players and the team owners lost because of the strike, but the players got hit the hardest. Yet, player representatives still thought they accomplished something, because before the strike they felt the players were the losers and the team owners were the winners. By striking, they lost even more, but at least they had the satisfaction of dragging the team owners into the loser bracket with them. This is sometimes referred to as the "crab pot theory": if you dump crabs in a big pot, occasionally one crab manages to scramble to the edge of the pot. However, before it escapes, the other crabs invariably grab it with their pincers and drag it back down to the bottom of the pot.

Be subtle. Pummeling people with contentious, overpowering broadsides backfires. Regardless of how brilliant your argument is, if you piss people off in its delivery, you will lose in the end. As William Buckley once remarked, "My general feeling is skill in formal argument hurts one in personal and business life, in that it encourages adversary postures where conciliatory postures are indicated."

Use the sound bite principle. The average person's attention span is pitifully short. It starts to fade after only 20 minutes, even if the person is intensely interested in the subject matter. Utilize this in your dealings with people. Here are some useful tips from successful unreasonable people—namely, trial attorneys:

1. Listeners are most receptive to facts, ideas, and conclusions during opening statements.

2. Eighty percent of listeners form their final opinions after hearing opening arguments.

3. People tend to remember the first and last things they hear and forget what was said in the middle.

4. Eighty-five percent of what we learn comes through our sense of sight. Thus, visual presentations are more effective than verbal ones.

Acting unreasonable undoubtedly goes against everything you previously have been taught. Unreasonableness is one of our culture's most universally frowned upon behaviors. The fact that this is so, however, is good. A predisposition toward reason in this country is exactly what enables one to capitalize on doing the opposite. In many cultures, a person is expected to act unreasonable when negotiating or bargaining. In those places, it is such common behavior it no longer contains a competitive advantage. It merely keeps bargainers even with competitors. The opportunities are much greater in America, because there are still plenty of reasonable people to be taken advantage of.

THE SECOND COMING OF THE WOOLLY MAMMOTH

However, it is important that you learn the tactics that unreasonable people employ even if you have no stomach for being unreasonable yourself. Fortunately, being proficient at recognizing and countering irrational arguments is almost as worthwhile as utilizing the strategies themselves.

Never argue with stupid people. Being intelligent, you'll undoubtedly lower yourself to their level so you can communicate. Because of their experience at that level, stupid people will beat you in an argument every time.

Don Martin

CHAPTER 18

SEX AND THE

SMALL BUSINESS PERSON

Tell the children to leave the room. We're going to talk about S-E-X. Well, maybe not sex itself, but the stuff that leads up to it. The topic, to be precise, is conduct that may escalate into sexual involvement with employees and, in particular, employees of a small business.

What happens when several attractive people wind up working together eight hours a day, five days a week within the confines of a small business environment? Right. More often than not, sexual tension rears its horny head. The bittersweet torment of sexual feelings can be a tonic for those afflicted, but it can be bad business for the business itself if the owner is involved. If the business owner is one of those smitten, my message is simple: take a cold shower and say no!

The social network of the typical small business isn't large enough to handle romantic involvement between the owner and an employee. When it happens, pre–love-affair prosperity can deteriorate into post–love-affair austerity. Sexual tension develops into temptation and titillation, which grows into licentiousness and lechery, accompanied by adultery and cuckoldry, followed by alimony and palimony, resulting in bankruptcy and insolvency. In short, we've got ruination, with a capital *R*, right here, right now, in small business city.

The Kinsey Institute says many people fool around a little at one time or another. From what I've seen, small business people do a good job of holding up their end of the statistics. If it is possible that you personally might seek extracurricular sex, heed my advice: stay away from employees. This seems so self-evident it hardly appears worthy of mention. Except for one thing: it keeps happening. And when sex shows up in the business place, common sense flies out the window.

Nowadays, a new hazard exists in the age-old game of office hanky-panky. Sex discrimination suits. It is one thing to fool around with a willing participant, but if the target of your affections thinks you a creep, there may be grounds to sue for sexual harassment. I know of one poor fool who was nailed with an indecent liberties charge for giving a woman an unsolicited and unappreciated squeeze. In a business environment, physical expressions should be restricted to handshakes and pats on the back.

First of all, the feelings of romance may be unilateral and your amorous advances may be a turn-off. In this case, if you come on too strong, you may wind up laying the groundwork for a lawsuit. A whole new body of law has arisen that makes companies liable for damages resulting from sexual harassment and sex discrimination (Title VII of the 1964 Civil Rights Act and the Equal Employment Opportunity Commission). Consequently, legal problems may result if sleeping with the boss is perceived to be a condition for advancement. The scary thing is that these types of lawsuits depend largely upon the testimony of those personally involved. This means, more often than not, that the decision comes down to who is to be believed. Who is the more credible—the accuser or the accused? It's a subjective determination.

Not only is it unwise to hustle an employee, it is unwise even to spend an inordinate amount of time alone with a particular employee. This is why most male doctors have a female nurse present when they examine a female patient. Witnesses are good insurance.

Furthermore, even if you personally are innocent, your company can be sued for activities of company superiors that may be viewed as harassment or discrimination. To guard against this, attorneys advise employers to distribute manuals to all employees that outline company policy against sexual harassment and that describe procedures for submitting complaints.

Back to your own libido, let's assume no sexual harassment is involved and that a hot and heavy relationship just happens to happen between you and an employee. Assume he or she is a consenting adult, or even that it is the employee who initiates the affair. It is still bad for your business.

An employee who becomes the lover of the business owner is no longer just an employee and will no longer behave as one. The relationship also will affect the work of other employees, who are likely to feel jealous and resentful, especially if the owner promotes the favored employee unjustifiably. Imagine yourself at such a company. If you were a co-worker of the lover, wouldn't you feel cynical and disrespectful toward the business owner?

Other hazards exist. Employer-employee love affairs often lead to proprietary possessiveness. The business owner is liable to wind up with a new business partner as well as a new partner in romance—a partner who wants a share of the business's assets.

Office lovers usually come to know a great deal about the personal side of the business, the sorts of things you would just as soon be kept confidential—your personal financial status, for example. You will undoubtedly come to regret any shared intimacies when that inevitable day arrives when the romance breaks up. I shouldn't have to remind you that a broken love affair can cause intense feelings. As many a prominent celebrity will testify, mad, emotionally hurt "ex's" can turn into incredible blabbermouths. Jilted lovers are one of the greatest sources of tips the

IRS has. In addition, there is always the possibility that the jilted lover may wind up working for a competitor.

Keep in mind that the foregoing sermonette applies equally to both genders. The sexual revolution and our changing culture has caused women business owners to have the same problems as their male counterparts. I know of situations in which subordinate young men have been propositioned by their female bosses. So don't assume that this chapter's message is male-gender specific. Welcome to the modern world.

Listen to me, kids. Many's the fine business I've seen suffer because its owner became romantically involved with an employee. An attractive employee's close proximity is a strong temptation, granted, but take my advice: if you are going to play around, do it in someone else's ball park.

CHAPTER 19

HUMBUGGERY

A man who has never gone to school may steal from a freight car, but if he has a university education he may steal the whole railroad. Franklin D. Roosevelt

A person's business career inevitably includes periodic encounters with individuals whose stock in trade is humbuggery. Double-dealers skilled at making their way in the business world selling snares and delusions. Commonly known as con artists. Those foolish or careless enough to fall for their scams wind up with humbug bites. The best protection, of course, is to clothe one's self in skepticism underwear, a cynicism shirt, and pessimism pants.

Duplicity has existed forever, but it seems particularly prevalent in American business. The reason so many con artists are running around in business suits is that everything in our society has to be sold. In our system, goods and services don't get used by proclamation or custom or decree. People must be talked into buying and using a product. Consequently, as Daniel Boorstin put it,

> You have to put the best light on things in order to sell them, you become preoccupied with appearances, with what looks good or sounds good. You put a premium on the believable rather than the true.

Hence, the confidence man society, in which everyone strives to outhustle their neighbors. To the glibbest sales person goes the spoils. But there's a fine line separating sales puffery from horse pucky. The temptation to transmogrify the truth is strong when a vacation to Hawaii is on the line.

Is it true we live in a con-artist culture? Does commerce turn on fiction and manipulative skills? Is the key to success being the consummate trickster? It is tempting to think so. As an experienced old businessman once commented, "Frost, the business world runs on bullshit."

But that's overstating it. Mr. Slick can slide a long way on glitter and glitz, but, in the last analysis, con artists eventually paint themselves into a corner where they are called upon to actually deliver. That is when they usually decide to leave town (with their victims' money).

But what about the "conees"—the people whom con artists prey upon? To them, I say: Wise up! Nobody is going to walk into your life and make you rich. Watch yourself if someone approaches you saying that for a modest fee they will furnish you with secrets guaranteeing instant wealth. Hug your wallet if someone says, "Anyone can make a million!" or "You, too, can have all the money you need for the rest of your life!" or "Let me share some amazing wealth-building secrets!"

If someone advertises that you can become rich simply by following a magic formula, take it with many grains of salt. Let's face it, kids. There aren't many secrets in this world, and those who have them aren't anxious to cut you in on the deal.

People wanting to go into business for themselves are very susceptible to get-rich-quick schemes. Combine the chance of being in business for yourself with the promise of quick, easy money and you've got an irresistible sales pitch. It's irresistible even if you are already in business for yourself. Years of hard work, worries, and modest rewards make a small business person ripe for the-grass-is-greener pitch. Get-rich-quick fever is an insidious disease. By rights, the law ought to allow its victims the option of voiding signed documents by reason of temporary insanity.

Closely related to the con artist is the con artist's first cousin, the promoter. A promoter is a con artist who stays for dinner. Instead of inveigling you out of a quick buck and then catching the next freight out of town, a promoter peddles long-term investments. Promoters try to talk you into advancing money for investments that supposedly will produce future profits for you but will provide immediate profits for themselves. Promoters strive to infect you with the belief that you, via them, will become independent, healthy, wealthy, and wise.

The thing about promoters to keep in mind is that their proposals may be good deals or they may be bad deals, but, for damn sure, they are always good deals for the promoter. This, quite naturally, makes their judgment biased at best and fraudulent at worst.

Promoters and con artists usually suffer the occupational disease of habitually spending money faster than they can talk it out of the suckers—which is to say they usually are broke. Right up until the time they close their deal with you, that is. The way, then, to smoke out a phony from a legitimate business person is to ask one simple question: "How much money are *you* putting in this deal, Buster?"

If Buster actually coughs up as much cash as you, you've probably got yourself an honest deal. It may still be a bad deal, but at least it's an honest one. On the other hand, if Buster's funds are tied up in "non-liquid investments," or if he thinks his proposition is so valuable that no investment on his part is necessary, you'd better start looking at him through X-ray glasses.

Actually, the perverse skills required to be an effective promoter or con artist are something to marvel at. A good promoter can make people believe in fairy tales. That takes talent. Skillful practitioners have an almost snake-like ability to mesmerize people. This is why TV evangelism is such an attractive field. TV preacherdom is particularly appealing because its practitioners don't need a gimmicky product. Once on the airwaves, all they need is the charisma itself.

Every current business fad becomes fair game for promoters. For many people, not being "in" on today's "in thing" is the worst of all possible fates. Promoters know this. Every time a new fad comes along (tax shelters, Hawaii condo timeshares, venture capital syndications, real estate investment trusts, financial planning seminars, leveraged buy-outs, passive income generators, master limited partnerships, or what have you) it is sure to attract promoters like honey attracts bears.

Prior to passage of the 1986 Tax Reform Act, tax shelters were a popular promoter vehicle. People interested in tax shelters were in high tax brackets and earned big bucks. That made tax shelters doubly attractive. Not only were they a fashionable investment, they were a fad of the rich as well.

I remember one highly skilled promoter who talked his prey out of large sums of money to invest on their behalf in tax shelters. Some money actually was invested in a few real estate ventures, all of which turned out to be losers. But the biggest chunk of investors' money was used for travel and entertainment and "management" fees, plus the purchase of a few assets used primarily by the promoter—such as an airplane, a boat, and a beach cabin.

The promoter's wealthy investors loved him. He produced such great tax losses for them. Once in a while, some investors would get restless when they heard rumors of how their money was being spent. When this happened, the promoter would call a partnership meeting. He knew it was time to cast another spell. Just an hour or so of his obtuse, bombastic magic and they would return once again to the fold. It was five years before they woke up to the fact that they had been had. By that time, all of their funds had gone down a rodent hole and their tax losses became real losses.

Franchise operations are a fertile field for promoters. They are a natural for promoters because they can be put together mostly on paper. In addition, franchises have strong appeal for people who want to be in business for themselves, because they are a quick-and-easy way to get started. Many promoter-type franchises use multilevel distributorships, alias pyramid sales. This is a commercial adaptation of the old chain letter gimmick. It works like this:

The product can be anything—cosmetics, household supplies, books, whatever. The promoter charges you, say, $5,000 for the right to be a distributor of his or her products. As a distributor, you get a 30 percent sales commission. In addition, you have the right to sell distributorships to others. If you sell a distributorship, you receive one half of the new distributor's entry fee plus a small percentage of the distributor's sales. You may even receive a percentage of whatever distributorships the new distributor sells. In this fashion, a pyramid of several levels is created with small pieces of action filtering up to those at the top. As any fool can plainly see, all one needs to do to make $100,000 a year is sell 10 distributorships a year. Forget peddling the product. Just sit back and collect your cut from the eager beavers below you.

Of course, you can see the problem. Pretty soon everyone is running around selling distributorships instead of the product. This is fine, except that eventually there aren't any customers—there are only distributors. Suppose a person sells 10 distributorships every year, and each new distributor in turn sells 10 distributorships the following year, and so on. Here is how fast they grow:

Year	Number of Distributors
0	1
1	11
2	121
3	1,331
4	14,641
5	161,051
6	1,771,561
7	19,487,171
8	214,358,881
9	2,357,947,691
10	25,937,424,601

Within seven years, there are more than enough distributors to equal the combined populations of the states of New York and North and South Dakota. If you keep going to year 10, there will be more distributors than have ever been people on earth.

The vulnerability of people to being conned, duped, flim-flammed, fooled, fleeced, cheated, tricked, had, gulled, and hoaxed never ceases to amaze me. The humbug never wants for victims. If someone dangles a proposal in front of you promising instant wealth, keep reminding yourself that there are only two wealth-building secrets, if you want to call them that. The first is that you have to be willing to take a chance. Like the proverbial turtle, you never get anywhere unless you stick your neck out. When it's fourth down and one yard to go, you go for a Hail-Mary pass instead of dropping back 10 yards to punt. Wealth, in other words, is a direct function of the so-called risk-reward ratio. The greater the risks, the greater the potential reward.

The second secret is to use your imagination. Let it soar. As Elvis Presley once said, "If you're gonna get anyplace, you gotta be different." Very true.

THE SECOND COMING OF THE WOOLLY MAMMOTH

Applying Elvis's philosophy to business usually means thinking up some sort of low-cost process, product, service, or method that is not now being done. Whatever it is, it must be new-fangled enough to have an untapped market. By the time word of an existing product filters down to your level, it is usually too late. Imitating others merely sets up a head-knocking contest with established competitors plus all of the other Johnny-come-latelys climbing aboard the bandwagon. That is why copycats hardly ever prosper when a new product cat is let out of the bag.

What it boils down to is this: You can start a conventional business, plod along, and work hard. Chances are you won't get rich but you probably won't starve to death either. With a little luck you may wind up making a very comfortable living.

Or you can shoot the works and try to get rich quick. You can dream and scheme, wheel and deal, promote and risk all. You may make it big or you may fail. Statistics show that the latter is more likely, but at least you will have had your chance. For some people, that is all they ask. For them, it is better to have tried and lost than never to have tried at all. For the rest of us, it is best to play the percentages. The chance of surviving in a small business, mundane as it may seem, is much greater than hitting the long ball on a strike-it-rich scheme.

I realize that conservative advice like this is a lonely voice in the wilderness. The shouts and roars of the dare-to-be-great crowd are overpowering. Positive and optimistic messages always seem to drive out words of caution. People do so want to believe. Consequently, we pessimists play to empty houses. Fortunately, we do have one small satisfaction. In the end we are traditionally permitted to say, "I told you so."

CHAPTER 20

BEWARE THE MUGGER

IN WHITE-COLLAR CLOTHING

A square-headed, hard-working Swede,
Propelled by inordinate greed,
Mucked around in the cold
'Til he found some coarse gold
Then came back to town at full speed.

A lawyer with galvanized jaw,
Whose mode of procedure was raw,
Sent a thief out to jump
The rich claim of the chump
And stake it "according to law."

The Swede is now stretched on the rack,
And trying to get his claim back,
While the Court takes its time
To consider the crime
'Til the receiver fills up his long sack.
Sam C. Dunham

If I had been born unscrupulous, the knowledge and experience I have gained as a CPA could have made me wealthy by now. With less middle-class morality and more low-class effrontery, I could have become well fixed as a professional embezzler. I know one thing: if I were an embezzler, I would concentrate on small businesses, because they are very vulnerable to white-collar crime. To explain why, let me walk you through a hypothetical example. To catch a thief, you must think like a thief, so let's pretend that I have been possessed by evil spirits and have suddenly and without warning been transformed into a consummate embezzler. Cackling fiendishly, I am set loose to prey upon the business world. Here is how I would go about it. See if you can figure out how to stop me!

First, I find a job as the bookkeeper/office-manager for some successful small contractor. Most people despise book work, especially active types like contractors. The prevailing attitude of most contractors is, "I don't wanta have anything to do with the damn books. I turn all that crap over to my bookkeeper."

When they do find a good, competent bookkeeper, most contractors are only too happy to give him or her complete responsibility for all office details, including the accounting records. The only function the contractor retains is signing checks and once in a while looking at the accounts receivable list to see which customers haven't yet paid their bills. So, finding a job with broad accounting responsibilities is easy.

My first official act as the office manager is to get the outside CPA fired. CPAs aren't much of a hazard to resident embezzlers. Small business people usually don't pay their CPAs enough to spend much time on their accounts. Their aversion to professional fees lies somewhere between income taxes and traffic fines. Nevertheless, CPAs are an uncomfortable nuisance. Even though CPAs take the position they are not professionally responsible for catching crooks, they may accidentally stumble onto something. Besides, getting rid of them is easy.

I sidle up to the boss and say, "Look, why pay that damn CPA a fancy fee? He's not really doing anything for you. I can do everything he's doing and you're already paying me to be here full-time anyway." That is usually enough to get the CPA out of the picture. Now I have carte blanche control over the books.

My first official act as an embezzler is to dip into the petty cash fund. The company keeps several hundred dollars in an old shoe box for payment of small cash expenditures. I rip it off for $100 or so a week. The boss works the cash box over pretty good himself. It's filled with illegible receipts, cryptic notes, I.O.U.s, rubber bands, and chewing gum wrappers, so salting it with phony petty cash invoices is easy. Besides, I'm the one responsible for replenishing it with cash and accounting for disbursements.

Next, I order additional company credit cards. Since one of my duties is to open and distribute the mail, it is easy for me to intercept the new credit cards without the boss seeing them. I now use the credit cards for such things as my personal car expenses.

Under the company name, I start buying personal items from suppliers, such as materials for my new swimming pool. I pull the invoices for these items from the support attached to the suppliers' statements. Since I am the person responsible for checking accounts payable for supporting documentation, the missing invoices are never noticed. So far, everything has been easy. To make things interesting, I indulge in a little petty thievery by taking postage stamps and tools home at night in my briefcase.

Now I get down to serious business. I open a separate company bank account in a strange bank some distance away—except I represent myself to that bank as the company's president and authorized check signer. Then I rent a couple of post office boxes to use as addresses for the fictitious suppliers' invoices I have printed up. I also set up bank accounts for these phony companies in other banks. Now I am ready to work my employer over as he sits there, fat, dumb, and happy, relieved that a good detail man is running his office.

When things get busy and the boss is running around trying to manage several different jobs at once, I type up some phony suppliers' invoices. I slip them in with the legitimate invoices left on his desk to be paid. It isn't likely, but should he happen to question one of them, I fire back with something like, "Oh, that's some stuff for the school job we worked on last month." The boss is too busy to check any explanation that sounds halfway reasonable, so he lets it pass. I deposit the checks for the phony invoices in my phony company bank accounts. Later, I transfer the funds to my personal account.

Every once in a while, money comes in from an old account receivable previously written off the books as a bad debt. I deposit these checks in my account, as well. There is no control over old accounts previously charged to bad debts, so nobody notices.

When the boss gets frantically busy, I walk into his office and say,

"Hey, Harry, how about signing some checks for me? I have to pay the bills today."

"Dammit, I'm busy! How many do you need?" I pretend to figure for a few seconds, "Let's see, we've got to pay the telephone bill, the lumber company, the plumber, . . . oh, I guess 15 will do."

Actually, I need only 14. The 15th pre-signed blank check I make out to myself for a substantial amount of cash. I enter it in the cash journal as having been for materials and supplies. There is no need to concern myself with destroying the evidence (the cashed check), because the boss's bank, like most others these days, no longer returns canceled checks to customers. My dirty deed lies buried in several miles of bank microfilm, like a grain of sand on Waikiki Beach, which is exactly where I intend to spend the money as soon as winter arrives.

Every month customers mail in payments to be applied to their accounts. I always keep several of these checks. I enter them in the accounts receivable records all right, but I juggle receivable and sales journal totals with adjustments to make them balance with cash. Since I have complete control over the mail, the bank deposits, the cash receipts journal, and the accounts receivable records, no sweat. My additions in the original books of record are never checked, so I sleep soundly at night.

The fact that some of these records are in a computer makes it simple, because computer-generated figures are easier to "cook" than hand-posted records. I have complete control over the computer as well as its input. The boss doesn't even know how to turn it on, let alone understand how it works. To him, it's a tool of the devil. He even has difficulty reading computer printouts because of their computerese format.

Sometimes, when a job superintendent phones in that a guy on one of the jobs has quit, I keep the terminated employee on the payroll for an extra week, except I take the guy's check and fraudulently endorse it over to myself. Since I pass out payroll checks for distribution to employees, it is easy for me to retain the phonies. The turnover among construction workers is normally very high. When you have 50 to 100 people working at times on several jobs, it is next to impossible for the boss to keep track of them all or to remember their names.

Once in a while, though, when the boss is signing payroll checks, he may hit me with, "Hey, I thought this guy quit?" I come over and look at the check and say, "Yeah, he quit the end of last week. He still had some time coming. He wants us to mail it to him." (The company pays employees the following week for the previous week's work.)

The boss acknowledges my explanation with a grunt and signs the check. I only sweat a little bit while this is going on. If he had pressed me on it, I would have taken the check back and said I would investigate it. Then I would get busy doing something else and tear it up later.

Now I present my own salary check for the boss's signature. My payroll check stub shows $2,000 gross, $500 withholding, and $1,500 net pay for the month. That is what I get paid, all right, so he signs it. Only, I don't enter it that way in the payroll journal. In the journal, I increase gross wages by $1,000 (a debit) and increase income tax withheld by $1,000 (a credit). Everything balances and net wages agree with cash disbursements. I'm the one who prepares the quarterly payroll tax returns, so I report it that way to the government. As a result, the company deposits an extra $1,000 of withholding tax for me every month. At year end, the company's computer prepares my annual W-2 form showing both my gross wages and withholding overstated by $12,000 (12 months at $1,000 per month). I file my tax return and get a refund of $8,640. (I don't get the full $12,000 back because including this amount in my gross income increased my income tax.)

The boss worries quite a bit about why he isn't making much money. "Damn unions keep upping their wages, damn suppliers keep increasing their prices, and the damn government takes everything that's left over. It's getting to where a man can't make an honest living anymore."

But suddenly the boss is saved! Just before he is about to declare bankruptcy, a good spirit comes along and transforms me back into an ethical CPA. I make full restitution of the stolen funds and tell the boss to let that be a lesson to him. (I like happy endings, don't you?)

You think the foregoing scenario is farfetched? Well, I have seen every one of those embezzlement techniques, or a variation thereof, perpetrated on someone at one time or another. White-collar criminals rob companies of billions of dollars every year—far more than burglars, purse snatchers, and shoplifters. Bank robbers, for example, only get four percent of the money stolen from banks. The other 96 percent is taken by trusted employees! Small businesses are particularly susceptible to embezzlement, because they usually have poor internal control.

THE SECOND COMING OF THE WOOLLY MAMMOTH

Internal control is accounting terminology for methods used to prevent a company's assets from being ripped off. There are two basic principles to good internal control:

1. Separation of duties between employees, and

2. Checking and verifying records

You will notice in my hypothetical embezzlements that I had complete control over the records, all the way from creating basic source documents to preparing financial statements and everything in between. There was no separation of accounting duties between different individuals. Also, no one ever checked my work—not even test-checked it. Naturally, the boss got embezzled. His lack of internal control was an open invitation. If I hadn't embezzled, someone else most likely would have come along later and done so. The situation described is common among small businesses.

Typically, a small business owner has had Trusty Tim or Faithful Mabel in the back room doing the company's books for the past 15 years or so. The owner just knows that this person is as honest as the day is long. And chances are that is a correct assumption. Most people basically are pretty honest. But even honest people will steal if they are overwhelmed by a personal financial crisis—particularly if they are reasonably sure they won't get caught, and especially if their dishonest behavior can be rationalized: "I was only borrowing it temporarily," "I needed it worse than the company," or "I was treated so rotten they had it coming."

So, cut embezzlers off at the pass. Don't provide them with the opportunity. Have good internal controls and try to provide support for employees with personal problems. Divide accounting duties among several people so it takes collusion to conceal hanky-panky. Have everyone's work checked and reconciled.

Suppose, in my example, someone else in the company recorded receipts and made bank deposits. It wouldn't be so easy to take money then, would it? Suppose job invoices required the approval of a job foreman or the boss before payment? Suppose someone else did the bank reconciliations? Suppose payroll checks were accompanied by employee time cards previously approved by job foremen? Suppose additions in hand-posted records were test-checked and detailed receivable lists were balanced to receivable control figures? Suppose computer totals were checked against input document batch totals? Suppose more than one person had access to and knowledge of the computer?

If these things were done, it would be hard for an employee to embezzle. Not impossible, but hard. That, however, is all you are really after. A dedicated embezzler usually can steal even under tight internal control. Internal control, for example, won't prevent crooked kickbacks from vendors to employees. But there are very few dedicated embezzlers around. Most are opportunists. If they have to work hard to embezzle, they won't.

How can you have tight internal control when you have a small company? How can you segregate duties with only one office employee? The answer is that you, the owner, must step in and become part of the office and an unofficial auditor. Small business owners can exercise considerable internal control even if they have no formal accounting training. Doing nothing more than evidencing a keen interest in the books will scare away most potential embezzlers.

Here are some things that business owners themselves can do that will provide good internal control:

1. Open the mail and make a list of cash received before turning it over to the bookkeeper.

2. Subsequently trace the list to the cash receipts journal.

3. Personally sign all checks, but only after they've been completed properly.

4. Personally approve and cancel all documentation in support of disbursements.

5. Review the bank reconciliation. Better yet, do the bank reconciliation yourself once in a while.

6. Require that monthly statements be sent on all delinquent receivables, and review them before they are sent out.

7. Personally approve accounts receivable adjustments and discounts.

8. Periodically test-check accounts payable statements to supporting invoices.

9. Personally approve, sign, and distribute all payroll checks.

10. Become personally acquainted with the company's fixed assets.

11. Become computer literate and knowledgeable enough to be able to access computer files and look things up yourself.

12. Periodically supervise a physical inventory of stock and materials.

13. Make sure that all employees take vacations and that employees who handle funds are bonded—particularly Trusty Tim and Faithful Mabel.

14. Require that cash sales be controlled by cash register tapes or locked counter receipt boxes that are reconciled to bank deposits.

15. Have an outside accountant come in periodically to review the books and test-check the records.

16. Take note of radical changes in employee life-styles.

17. Do background checks on prospective employees.

18. Let employees know you have an open door policy for discussing their personal problems.

I know from experience that you won't do all of these things. Many of you won't bother doing any. A few of you will perform some, get bored, and quit. But don't say I didn't warn you. By the way, you don't need a good bookkeeper, do you?

CHAPTER 21

THE LAW OF LEAST BUNGLES

If at first you don't succeed, try, try again. Then quit.
There's no sense being a damn fool about it. W. C. Fields

Every enlisted man knows that armies don't win wars because of the brilliance of their commanders. Rather, one army wins because it happens to commit fewer bungles than the other.

Every week, half of America's football coaches flagellate themselves, telling sports reporters, "We beat ourselves with our own mistakes."

Every losing politician knows deep down that he or she would be ensconced in City Hall right now if it weren't for his or her campaign manager's errors.

There is a common thread running throughout here. The success of human enterprise is a function of the mistakes made rather than the quality of the strategy employed. The same principle found in war, sports, and politics also applies to business.

Hence, Frost's *law of least bungles:* The success of a business is inversely proportional to the weight of its accumulated bungles. As Yogi Berra once said, "We made too many wrong mistakes!"

The law of least bungles can be expressed quantifiably as follows:

$$\text{bungle value (B)} = \dfrac{\dfrac{1}{t_2}}{\dfrac{1 - (\text{sum bm}) \times (1/M)}{t_1}}$$

Where: (sum bm) is a mathematical expression representing the sum of the bungle masses (bm), or detrimental effects, of all of the bungles made in a business from time (t_1) to time (t_2). When this term reaches the business's critical mass (M), the formula reduces to: $B = 1/0 = \infty$ (infinity)—an impossible situation, which means that particular business ceases to exist!

Every individual bungle has a certain amount of detrimental effect on a business person's situation. The detrimental effects of many bungles accumulate like radioactive sludge. Small businesses are highly unstable affairs. When the weight of their accumulated bungles reaches critical mass, the businesses self-destruct.

Most small business people intuitively recognize this. Unfortunately, this leads them into a faulty decision-making habit. Knowing intuitively that big, important decisions have large amounts of potential bungle mass associated with them, the average person puts off making major decisions for fear of the consequences should he or she screw up.

This is why most people concentrate on piddly, unimportant decisions rather than on big ones. They'll spend more time making sure secretaries don't waste paper clips than they will modernizing their production line. More thought goes into purchasing the boss's car than in analyzing the company's financial statements. Planning the annual Christmas party receives more attention than revamping the company's sales and distribution system.

What these people fail to realize is that not making a decision is a decision itself. Ignoring an important decision leaves it to chance. Depending upon the vagaries of chance is more likely to cause bungling than stepping up to the line and making the decision yourself. With a little experience, the average business person can make the right decision approximately 59.5 percent of the time. That might not seem like much improvement over the 50-50 laws of chance, but it still gives you an advantage over most other operators. Bungling, after all, is relative. To be successful over one's competitors, one only need have a lower bungle value than they.

This brings me to the subject of "rearorities." Most people have little difficulty establishing a list of priorities. The problem the average small business person has is not having enough time to take care of everything regardless of priority. Even when they are high on the priority list, some problems have to be ignored altogether. Deciding which to ignore is far harder than merely listing them in order of significance. Small problems can be more unpleasant emotionally than large ones. So most small business people utilize the "squeaky wheel" method of problem solving. They focus on what is bouncing up and down in front of them making the most noise at the moment.

A more logical way to operate is to create a list of "rearorities." List problems that, consciously and purposely, you are going to let go to hell. Problems at the top of your list will be the ones you are not going to bother with. When you run short of time during the day, consult your "rearority" list for things you aren't going to get done.

Of course, to do this, you must gird yourself and steel your mind against all the squeaks and screams that neglected small problems will make. This is not an easy thing to endure. Occasionally, you may have to give in to one or two of them just for peace of mind. Otherwise, a stream of neglected small problems turns into Chinese water torture.

Many people overlook this concept because Frost's law of least bungles is a law of accretion, with a slow, cumulative effect. People don't notice their accumulated bungles until an overload of bungle mass builds up. The impact of large, silent problems goes unnoticed because people are distracted by all of the small, noisy difficulties besetting them. Unnoticed, that is, until the inevitable day arrives when the advancing glacier of big problems blocks their front door.

In addition, people quite naturally favor spending time doing things they enjoy rather than tasks they consider disagreeable. Everybody knows the typical small business person wears many hats. What most people don't think about is how to decide which hat to put on next. Wake up most small business people in the morning and ask them what needs their personal attention during the day and they probably will rattle off a number of items. Next, ask them the order in which they are going to deal with those matters. After that, ask them to rank the tasks in order of disagreeableness. What do you want to bet their priority list and disagreeableness list are in inverse order?

Bingo. We've hit once again upon one of the biggest failings found in small business—doing what you like to do best rather than doing what most needs to be done. Acting this way is perfectly natural. Acting contrariwise is perfectly unnatural. And that is why utilizing Frost's law of least bungles represents a golden opportunity: most people take the easy way out and instinctively refuse to act in a manner contrary to their basic human nature.

If, through enlightened will power, you deal with matters according to their bungle value, you will automatically achieve an edge. So, take advantage of the law of least bungles. Spend time on problems based upon their bungle value rather than their noisiness or your comfort level. Decrease your accumulated bungle mass by not leaving big problems to chance. Adhere to these few principles and you will undoubtedly wind up in front of the pack.

The Prisoner's Dilemma
Two burglars are being interrogated by the police in separate rooms. The evidence against them won't support a conviction unless they confess. The detective tells each in private he will go free if he confesses and squeals on his companion. If he doesn't confess but his partner does, he will get 10 years. Finally, if both confess and implicate each other, they each will get five years.

Each confesses and rats on the other, thereby getting five years. Sound stupid? Sure, but in terms of personal self-interest there is logic behind their decision.

From the point of view of each burglar, not confessing means he either goes free or gets 10 years. On the other hand, if he confesses and rats on his companion, he goes free or gets five years. Clearly, freedom or five sounds better than freedom or 10, so they become stool pigeons and sing like canaries.

The same dilemma confronts business people. Suppose you stand to make

$10,000 bidding normal prices on a job. However, if you don't get the bid, you will lose $5,000 because of overhead and equipment payment commitments. Bidding low, you are assured of being awarded the job, but the best you could do then is to break even. People in this situation often get trapped by the "prisoner's dilemma." They bid low because they would rather be certain of breaking even than try to make $10,000 and risk losing $5,000.

from Heavy Stomachs   Edmond York

CHAPTER 22

THE ADVANTAGES OF RIOTOUS LIVING

Business and financial consultants tell people to keep personal living expenses low when starting a new business. Live frugally, they say, and plow the savings back into your business.

Nonsense. Counterintuitive as it may seem, you should do just the opposite. Live high on the hog. Accumulate car and country club payments. Go on expensive trips. Live in a big house and buy expensive furniture. Take big draws out of your business to cover it all.

Soon, your business will come under severe financial pressure. Beginning capital normally will be limited to what you can scrape up personally and what you can wheedle out of the bank. When this money is dissipated by high living expenses, your fledgling business will quickly run short of working capital. Contrary to traditional wisdom, this is a desirable state of affairs! There is nothing so stimulating as a big pile of bills and no money in the bank. Once the desperateness of the situation sinks in, you will, in your terror, rise to heights never before dreamed of. You will unwittingly have unleashed the reservoirs of incentive and drive lying dormant within your soul. These are the strongest assets anyone can ever have. True, you risk disaster and bankruptcy if you use this approach to summon them. But think how effective you will be after they arrive.

He who survives being chased by the hounds of financial hell will turn into a sound business person. Prior calamities have molded some of the most capable small business people I know. For one thing, survivors of financial crises become very cost conscious. Nobody sells them any frills. It is basic necessities, period. Survivors of near bankruptcy turn into hard heads. It isn't easy to fool such people; they have heard it all before. They become cynical and pessimistic, which makes for a more realistic outlook on business affairs. Finally, after a few narrow escapes, a person invariably comes to appreciate the smaller things in life. A few close calls beget humility and perspective. People become more content with their lot in life, knowing that, but for the grace of God and a little bit of luck, they could be much worse off than they are today. Revelations like this create human happiness—plus more intelligent management of a small business.

CHAPTER 23

THE SONG OF THE FRANCHISE SIREN

If you surprise an intruder in the act of burglarizing your home, do not panic. Remember, he is as frightened as you are. One good device is to rob him. Seize the initiative and relieve the burglar of his watch and wallet. Then he can get in your bed while you make a getaway. Trapped by this device, I once wound up living in Des Moines for six years with another man's wife and three children, and only left when I was fortunate enough to surprise another burglar who took my place. Woody Allen

Next, ladies and gentlemen, by popular demand and in response to the fervid desires of all those thousands everywhere who want to be in business for themselves, let me present the Franchise Siren! Listen to her now as she sings her sweet song of opportunity while sidling up to a franchise prospect (accompanied by the soothing sounds of big business violins playing in the background):

Hello, there, good-lookin'! How'd you like to be in business for yourself? How'd you like to be your own boss? Come on, aren't you tired of the same old rat race? Follow me. I'll set you up in a business of your very own. It's simple. It's easy. I'll take care of everything. I'll give you a product to sell; I'll find you a location; I'll have a building constructed and see that you have the latest equipment; I'll give you tried-and-true procedures to follow (free, at no extra cost); I'll train you, advise you, advertise, help you find financing, and I'll hold your hand. All you have to do is be the boss and collect all the money!

THE SECOND COMING OF THE WOOLLY MAMMOTH

Just cash in your savings, get a loan at the bank, mortgage yourself to the hilt, pay me a modest fee, give me a small piece of the action, buy all of your supplies from me, sign this simple little contract agreeing to do everything my way, and you'll finally be in business for yourself. Isn't this a great opportunity? This offer can't last, so you'd better sign quick before some other lucky dog gets me!

Pardon me for letting my cynicism show. I guess I've seen too many phony franchise deals in my time. At first glance, franchise operations look like a sound concept. Some are. But running a franchise operation is not really the same as being in business for yourself. From a practical standpoint, it is more like you are buying yourself a job with responsibilities—sort of a branch managership. True, as a franchisee, you have a certain amount of autonomy. But your modes of operation are severely restricted by the franchisor's regulations.

Franchises work this way: The franchise company (franchisor) has a prominent name and symbol. It sells the right to use these intangible assets in a particular location for a fee. The buyer (franchisee) agrees to pay a percentage of the income (royalties) to the parent company. The franchisee usually has to buy certain key ingredients and supplies from the parent company. In return, the franchisee has the right to use the franchisor's well-established trade name and trade-tested (supposedly) marketing techniques. The franchisee also is supposed to receive training, management advice, pooled advertising, and assistance with financing equipment and facilities.

The beauty of this, as far as the franchise company is concerned, is that it can expand rapidly with little of its own capital. The individual franchisees provide the expansion money. By not having to issue additional capital stock, no dilution of ownership occurs. The leverage is tremendous. In addition, since franchisees have their own money invested, they presumably will operate in a prudent and conscientious manner.

The advantage for franchisees is they are theoretically in business for themselves. Yet, they have the protective umbrella of a big parent company over them.

Although franchising is not exactly the same as being in business for yourself, perhaps it may be thought of as a compromise—a sort of halfway house. However, be careful! The franchise concept attracts con artists, flim-flammers, and rip-off artists. When considering a franchise proposition, for heaven's sake, investigate it thoroughly. Here is a checklist of the sorts of questions you should ask yourself when considering a franchise:

1. Has your lawyer examined the franchise contract?

2. Does the franchise involve anything considered illegal or questionable in your locality? (A divorce service franchisee got himself in a pickle because nobody told him that advertising divorce services was illegal in his state.)

3. Have you had an accountant analyze the financial projections and prepare a budget? Have you checked comparative prices of supplies required to be bought from the parent company?

4. Will you have an exclusive territory?

5. Is the franchisor connected with any other company handling a similar product or service? If so, what protection do you have against competition from the second firm?

6. Under what circumstances can you get out of the franchise contract, and what will it cost if you do?

7. How many years has the franchise company been in business, and does it have certified financial statements? If so, how sound is the company financially?

8. Does the franchise company provide:
   a. Management training?
   b. Employee training?
   c. Public relations and advertising?
   d. Capital?
   e. Credit?
   f. Merchandising ideas?
   g. Help in finding a location?
   h. Help constructing the facility?

9. Are you ready to give up some of your independence for the security of the franchise?

10. Are you ready to spend the rest of your business life with the franchisor and its product?

11. What can the franchisor do for you that you cannot do for yourself?

Another important thing you should do is to check with people already operating one of the franchises. Ask them if they are making as much money as the franchisor estimated. Ask them what sort of help they were provided and whether the franchise company lived up to its agreements.

For information regarding specific franchise companies, write the U.S. Department of Commerce, Washington, D.C. for its publication, *Franchise Company Data,* which is also available through U.S. Government Printing Office bookstores. And beware of the franchise siren who sings but doesn't deliver.

PART FOUR

THE ''F'' WORD (FINANCES)

CHAPTER 24

THE WONDERS OF O.P.M.

Money doesn't grow on trees, and if it did, someone else would own the orchard.   Lewis Grizzard

A client entered my office one day with a big grin on his face. "Why are you so happy, Sam?" I asked.

"I just got through closing a real estate deal," replied Sam. "I came out all right on it, too," he added, as he tossed the closing statement for the sale onto my desk.

I congratulated him and began perusing the figures. "I see you sold the property for $100,000," I said, "but how much did it cost when you bought it?"

"I paid $50,000 cash for it four years ago. It was a vacant building lot. I had some extra money at the time, so I decided to put it into real estate. Sure glad I did. A 100 percent profit isn't too bad, is it?"

"No, it isn't," I replied, "except it took four years to materialize."

"Okay," said Sam, "divide 100 percent by four years and I made 25 percent per year. That's still a pretty good profit, isn't it?"

"Absolutely," I said, "except you didn't make 25 percent either. That calculation doesn't take into account what your $50,000 would have earned during the time it was tied up in real estate. In other words, you aren't allowing for the time value of money."

"Well," said Sam (who by now was getting a little annoyed at my cold water treatment), "how much would it be on a time-value-of-money basis?"

"That depends upon what your $50,000 would have earned elsewhere.

Financial experts use something called the *internal rate of return* in situations like this to come up with a more realistic measure of return."

"Fine. So how do I calculate my internal rate of return?"

"It's rather complicated because it involves present value calculations. However, my financial calculator contains the appropriate formulas, so I can figure it out in a minute or two."

"Fantastic," said Sam. "What, pray tell, does it turn out to be?"

I went through the calculations. "It's less than the 25 percent you thought you made. It's 19 percent."

Sam looked somewhat deflated but was still in good spirits, so I continued on. "Let me ask you something, Sam. Instead of paying all cash for the property, suppose you had made a $10,000 down payment and signed a 15-year, 10 percent contract for the $40,000 balance. Suppose you had made annual contract payments over the four years and then sold the property for $100,000. What do you think your rate of return would be on a deal like that?"

"I imagine it would be less because my profit would be less. I would have paid a big chunk of interest on the real estate contract before I sold the property."

I made a few more calculations on my calculator. "It is true your profit would be less. Your payments on the contract would be $5,258 per year. After four years, you would have paid $15,194 of interest. That would reduce your $50,000 profit down to $34,806."

"I told you so," said Sam, with a triumphant look on his face. "It takes money to make money."

"But you are overlooking something," I said, trying hard not to sound too patronizing. "Buying the lot on contract means you would have invested only $25,774 of your own money to earn the $34,806 profit—a $10,000 down payment and three contract payments of $5,258, assuming you sold the property at the same time the fourth year payment was due. Investing less cash and spreading your cash over four years would have made a big difference on your rate of return."

"Okay, I'll bite," said Sam, "what kind of internal rate of return would that have been?"

I made the calculations. "It would have been 34 percent. That is 15 percentage points higher than the 19 percent you received by paying all cash for the property. Your $50,000 would have been enough to buy two lots on a contract basis. Two lots would have generated nearly $70,000 of profit instead of $50,000."

Sam reviewed my calculations. "Very interesting," he mused. Then he looked at me and said with a sly grin, "Since you have succeeded in putting a damper on what a few minutes ago was my moment of triumph, I will consider this to be a courtesy conference when you send your next bill."

Sam had just been initiated into the secret "O.P.M. Club." (O.P.M. stands for "other people's money" and is commonly known as leverage.) O.P.M. is the stock-in-trade of all big-time promoters. By financing investments with other peoples' money, you introduce a multiplier effect on the profits your investment makes. This happens because you own 100 percent of the profits (after interest expense), regardless of how little you yourself invest. Furthermore, by spreading out your funds as down payments in numerous projects, you expand the scope of your investing and multiply your profits even more.

As an additional bonus, O.P.M. takes advantage of inflation, because, to the extent that inflation occurs, loans will be repaid with less valuable dollars. At current rates, loan repayment dollars will erode five percent or so every year. On top of that, interest expense is tax-deductible against the income the investment earns, which means that Uncle Sam subsidizes your interest expense.

Sounds like a heck of a way to make money, doesn't it? It is, which is why so many sharpies utilize leverage in their financial dealings. You, too, can cash in on this principle by applying it to your own business. By using borrowed money, you can multiply the rate of return on your own capital investment—assuming, that is, you are capable of earning a higher rate of return than the interest rate being paid on the borrowed money.

Of course, there is one little thing you do have to be very careful of. Leverage multiplies in reverse if a project fails! If your own $10,000 completely pays for an investment that goes sour, all you lose is $10,000. However, suppose you leverage by borrowing an additional $90,000 to make a $100,000 investment. Now, if the investment fails, not only is your $10,000 lost, you also have to pay the $90,000 you borrowed, plus accumulated interest. Instead of being a financial fat cat, you are a destitute dog.

Furthermore, once word gets out on the street that you are having financial problems, the credit vultures will descend. Other people to whom you owe money might get nervous and call their loans as well. The domino theory is a fact of life in the world of O.P.M. This is why every time recession shakes the economic tree, the air is filled with over-financed promoters falling off the limbs they were perched on. (Duck! Here comes Donald Trump!)

Nevertheless, leverage within reason makes sense. This needs to be emphasized because many people have hang-ups about borrowing. There are business people walking around whose companies could benefit from borrowed money and could qualify for loans, but these people are reluctant to go that route. Better their businesses should suffer from under-financing than that they borrow on their life insurance or remortgage their homes or factor their receivables at the bank. For them, borrowing is an evil practice.

Many suppliers give discounts for prompt payment. Common terms allow a two percent discount if the customer pays within 10 days of invoice; otherwise, payment is due within 30 days. That two percent might not look like much, but it is an effective rate of 36 percent over the 20 days from the end of the discount period (the 10th day) and the 30th day, when the invoice is due. Furthermore, many suppliers charge an extra one percent or two percent if you go past 30 days. That amounts to 18 percent yearly interest. Yet, the small business person who borrows to make discounts or to avoid late charges is a rare bird.

So, don't be hobbled by old-fashioned inhibitions against borrowing. Have enough self-confidence to use O.P.M. No one is going to loan you money unless they believe that either you or the underlying security will repay them. The faith you have in yourself should at least equal that of your creditors. Otherwise, you have no business being in business.

CHAPTER 25

HARVESTING MONEY TREE FRUIT

Money is always there but the pockets change, it is not in
the same pockets after a change, and that is all there is to
say about money.   Gertrude Stein

Now that I've convinced you that using O.P.M. is a sound business practice, how does one get some? Let's look at possible sources.

Suppose some strangers sidle up to you and say, "Here's a million dollars. Take it. Use it in your business any way you see fit—no strings attached. We are loaning you this money, but don't bother paying us back.
And we will leave it up to you as to whether you pay us any interest."

A far out fantasy? No. This happens every time a corporation floats a
public stock issue. From a practical standpoint, money received from
capital stock is like having a permanent loan. It never has to be repaid.
The only costs are whatever dividends the company decides to distribute. However, there is no requirement that any be paid. Dividends usually are kept at a low rate or are made in the form of additional shares of
capital stock rather than cash. This is why stockholders of large publicly
held corporations expect to make money from appreciation in their
stock's value rather than from cash dividends.

Unfortunately, selling stock is not a practical possibility for small,
closely held companies. Who would ever think of buying stock in the
corner deli or the local laundry? Usually, only large, well-established
companies can obtain investment capital by issuing capital stock.

Large corporations have other fund sources not accessible to small
companies. They can issue debenture bonds. Debentures are better

than stock in one respect, because ownership of the company isn't diluted. This creates leverage. But money from bonds does have to be repaid, including interest. However, maturity dates are long-term; 10-year repayment schedules are common. Best of all, unlike most other loans, debenture bonds are unsecured. The corporation doesn't have to tie up its assets as collateral. But who in their right mind would buy bonds issued by a small, closely held corporation?

Ever wonder what happens to the premiums you pay on your life insurance policies? Most of this money is held in reserve for future losses and claims. Insurance companies earn income on these reserves by loaning money to large businesses, usually for terms of 10 to 15 years. Guess who has access to this vast source of capital? It isn't the Ajax Roofing Company of Elephant's Breath, Arizona. It isn't the Squeehawkin' Novelty and Variety Store, either.

Another advantage that large corporations enjoy is not having to kowtow to banks. Instead of going hat in hand—like you and me and other mortals—to borrow from banks, corporations can borrow direct by issuing what is known as *commercial paper.* These are short-term, unsecured promissory notes sold by large corporations in the open capital markets in denominations of $25,000 or more. Interest paid on commercial paper is usually comparable to prime.

What I'm pointing out here is that the money tree's juiciest fruit is too high up for most small businesses to reach. But there's no sense pining over it. Small business owners must accept reality and find what exists on the lower branches. Well, what is available to the little guy?

The primary source, of course, is the personal assets of the small business entrepreneur. So, before starting your business, accumulate as much money ahead of time as you can, because very likely that will be the extent of any long-term investment capital you scare up.

The other major source comes from the business pulling itself up by its bootstraps. In other words, it retains profits rather than distributing profits as bonuses or dividends. Unfortunately, profits can take a long time to build up, so expansion from this source can be a slow process.

Beyond this, you have to rely on your ingenuity, resourcefulness, and hustle. Let's not kid ourselves. It's tough out there, gang. But there are ways and means of coming up with small business financing. Here is a rundown of possibilities, starting with the most realistic sources—in other words, the most likely categories of financing.

1. Your Own Funds

Keep your overhead skinny. Stifle overhead costs, particularly at the outset. This goes without saying. For example, if possible, operate your business out of your own home. Allocate funds to assets that actually make you money rather than on the trappings. Buy top-of-the-line shop equipment instead of fancy office furniture.

Sell personal assets. Sell your boat and camper. You'll be too busy establishing your business to use them much, anyway.

Minimize personal living expenses. Go on an austerity program. Eat chicken instead of steaks. You'll lower your cholesterol level besides saving money.

Commit your savings and retirement funds. If you don't believe in your own ideas and abilities enough to invest personal savings, then there isn't much hope for your business.

Borrow against your home equity. This takes guts, because the home is usually a family's "sacred cow" security. But it is often the best collateral most people have and may be worth a significant amount.

Borrow against life insurance policies. Loans on the cash surrender value of life insurance policies are an excellent source of financing, and interest rates are reasonable.

2. Outside Sources of Income

Have your spouse work. This could make all the difference in the world, because it could enable the entrepreneur to plow his or her own salary back into the business.

Employ your kids instead of outsiders. Your children could be a source of reliable part-time help, which may spare you the expense of hiring full-time employees.

Moonlight with a second job. This is a last resort, because it would interfere with your new enterprise. On a temporary basis, though, it may be a way to get started.

3. Silent Partners

A silent partner is someone who invests but doesn't actively participate in the business. I don't encourage this source, because a silent partner won't know what's going on day-to-day, which can generate unfounded suspicions and paranoid speculation, which, in turn, breeds friction. Plus, nobody can second-guess quite as well as a silent partner.

4. Friends and Relatives (A Last Resort)

I don't advise borrowing money from friends, unless you don't care whether they remain friends. Loans from relatives are also touchy arrangements. If you do borrow from these sources, keep it business-like: a formal promissory note with a firm repayment schedule, a realistic interest rate, and collateral, if possible.

5. Banks

Banks are small business's biggest source of working capital. They will be covered separately in the next chapter. For now, we'll just list the major types of bank loans.

- Receivable and inventory loans
- Term loans
- Flooring loans
- Lines of credit

6. Factoring

This is where you sell your receivables to a finance company. Factoring is expensive. Interest charges are heavy because the finance company assumes the burden and risk of collecting. Factoring has bad connotations, which might damage your reputation. Customers normally aren't too keen on having their accounts sold to a finance company. In addition, other creditors may take it as a sign you've fallen on hard times and may tighten up their own credit terms.

7. Long-Term Borrowing

Equipment loans. Equipment purchases can usually be financed for from three to six years, either by the equipment manufacturer or by a bank. The equipment itself serves as collateral via a chattel mortgage. Interest rates are normally high. Down payments of 20 percent to 33 percent are usually required.

Long-term mortgages. The idea here is to make business real estate investments as long-term as possible. In other words, go for the lowest down payment and the longest pay-back period you can get away with. You can always make extra payments if you become flush in the future.

8. Borrow from Uncle Sam

Small Business Administration (SBA) direct loans. SBA direct loan programs are still available for severely handicapped individuals, Vietnam vets, and entrepreneurs in high unemployment areas. Otherwise, the chances of obtaining a direct loan from SBA are slim to none.

SBA guaranteed loans. You have a better shot at sweet-talking SBA into guaranteeing a loan at the bank. This is possible if your business is too under-financed for the bank to stomach but legitimate enough for SBA to believe in. Some finance companies specialize in loaning mortgage money to small businesses guaranteed by SBA. The Money Store Investment Corporation is probably the largest. Because of SBA's guarantee, low down payments of 10 percent are available. However, interest rates are a point or so higher than regular commercial mortgages.

504 loans. So-called "certified development companies" are authorized by the government to sell debenture bonds guaranteed by SBA to provide funds for small business development loans. This loan money is earmarked for plant and equipment acquisitions that will generate additional employment. Up to 20-year, 90 percent financing is available under a 504 program, with the bank characteristically loaning about half and the certified development company the balance at rates somewhat lower than commercial interest. The only drawback is that you are locked in. A 504 loan cannot be paid off ahead of time without paying a substantial premium, because cash flow from the loan is needed to fund the underlying bond payments.

Small Business Innovation Research (SBIR) grants. If you have a red-hot idea for a new product, believe it or not, you may be eligible for a government research grant available through various government agencies. After you complete the research and development phase, SBIR grants sometimes provide funding for commercialization of the product. Check with SBA for details.

Export loans. If you are into exporting, government programs for small businesses exist through the Export-Import Bank (Eximbank) and the Overseas Private Investment Corporation (OPIC). They involve government guarantees of commercial export loans and insuring the value of overseas shipments. These serve as lubricant to grease the skids for the shipper's regular commercial borrowing. Your local SBA office can provide contact information.

Small Business Investment Companies (SBICs). SBICs are a semigovernment source of money. They are investment companies licensed by and operated under federal regulations to provide equity funds and development loans for small businesses. Half to two-thirds of their funds come from government sources, but they are owned by private investors and are run as profit-making ventures. Originally they seemed like a good idea. A source of risk capital for small business certainly is needed. Unfortunately, most have been financial disasters, so they are rare birds these days. The dealings my clients have had with SBICs have been expensive. Because of the horrendous history of bad debt losses that SBICs have had, they tend to require a pound of flesh, your first-born child, and a world series ticket before coughing up any funds. Check with SBA to see if any still exist in your area.

Quasi-governmental organizations. Some localities have Economic Development Corporations and Commercial Development Corpora-

THE SECOND COMING OF THE WOOLLY MAMMOTH

tions that provide a certain amount of financing. These are organizations sponsored in part by the government. Their purpose is to stimulate and aid private enterprise in areas deemed in need of economic stimulation. Your local SBA office can give you information as to whether any are located in your area.

9. Trade Borrowing

Get advance deposits from customers. In other words, ask for money up-front. This is an often overlooked source. It can be a big help if customers can be talked into doing it. As a matter of fact, it is standard practice in some industries, primarily those that involve sizable costs to service customers, such as construction of heavy equipment or the manufacture of substantial inventories.

Use suppliers' terms (90-day accounts). Sometimes major suppliers will help a new business get started by granting 90 days or more to pay instead of the normal 30 days. The hope is the fledgling company will eventually become a large customer. It is well worthwhile to hit up suppliers for extended credit. As the god of chutzpa says, "It never hurts to ask."

Use "trade" credit (delay paying your bills). Some business people borrow from suppliers and other creditors by paying late. But you can only work trade credit so far. It's usually only a few months before the creditors start hammering you for their money. But a few months' float may be all that's needed to keep your head above water.

10. Lease Borrowing

Rent facilities and equipment. You don't need as much of a down payment as with a straight purchase. However, interest costs built into equipment leases are higher than in normal borrowing. So, in the long run, leasing costs you more.

11. Tax Borrowing

Use the cash method of accounting (if you are eligible). This is where you elect to report taxable income based upon cash receipts rather than on accounts receivable. It is available only to smaller companies that don't have resale inventories as an income-producing part of their business. The advantage of cash basis accounting is that you defer paying tax on receivables until they are actually collected.

Use the corporate form of organization to take advantage of lower federal income tax rates. Corporate taxes are lower on the first $75,000 of taxable income than personal rates on the same amount of income. More on this later.

The following list outlines more exotic sources of financing. It is the slim-to-none category.

1. Wealthy Investors

Most wealthy individuals are conditioned to being constantly hit upon, so they are very guarded and hard to get to. Your best chance may be to find an ugly one and propose marriage.

2. Venture Capital Companies

These are partnerships of wealthy individuals set up to invest money in promising young businesses. Unfortunately, venture capitalists aren't interested unless the target company is in a glamour field (currently, high-tech stuff such as genetic engineering). They want young companies with big ideas that are only temporarily small during their start-up phase. In other words, they are looking for long-ball hitters—like another Apple Computer.

3. Public Stock Offerings

As previously indicated, selling stock to the public is viable only for large, mature companies. Actually, this isn't entirely true. Occasionally, a small business person does manage to peddle stock in a small, private offering. Even so, it is costly, because brokerage firms handling a small offering take big bites out of the proceeds to cover their costs. If you short-circuit brokers and try to sell stock on your own, check with your attorney first to make sure you are doing it in a legal manner. State and federal security laws are very restrictive. Normally, though, people aren't interested in becoming a minority stockholder in a small company, and with good reason. How do you cash in on stock of a company over which you have no control and for which there is no market?

4. Mergers

If worse comes to worse, hooking up with a larger, better established company offers a way out. However, letting yourself be swallowed up in a merger means losing your independence and freedom.

5. Venture Leasing

Because of the risks inherent in leasing expensive equipment to start up companies, some leasing companies will take an equity position in a new company to sweeten the deal. The problem, of course, is this dilutes the entrepreneur's profit. However, if it enables you to get started when otherwise you wouldn't, then 50 percent of something is better than 100 percent of nothing.

6. Foreign Investors

This is a practical possibility only for certain specialized industries doing business overseas, such as fishing, clothing manufacture, and raw materials mining. Foreign investment also happens sometimes in real estate ventures. Some port authorities have established free trade zones for commercial activities involving foreign companies. You might nose around them for contacts.

7. Sharks

Stay away from loan sharks and organized crime money. Not only are interest rates high, nonpayment of their loans can be detrimental to your health. It's hard to operate a business when your legs are broken.

That's about it. As you can see, small business has a problem. Most of its money sources involve high interest costs and short repayment terms.

But don't get discouraged. Be persistent. If your proposal is viable, you may eventually come up with something if you just keep jumping at the money tree fruit.

The world's most famous famous last words:
> *I never—I always*
> *I can't—I can*
> *I won't—I will*
> *I don't—I do*

Moral: Avoid absolutes. It won't do if you can't but can, and it never will if you don't always.

CHAPTER 26

YOUR FRIENDLY BANKERS—

HAL AND FRANK

Except for con men borrowing money they shouldn't get and widows visiting handsome young men in the trust department, no sane person ever enjoys visiting a bank. Martin Mayer

Jesus had the right idea when he drove the money changers from the temple. I've never much cared for bankers either. Bankers loan you an umbrella when the sun is shining and take it away when it rains. I've often thought if I had all of them in a big gunny sack on a boat out in the middle of the ocean, I would jump overboard with the sack and sacrifice myself just to rid the world of them.

I shouldn't be so hard on bankers, because they have an awesome responsibility. They are small business's major source of outside capital, which is a big problem these days. As everyone knows, America's banking system is in the soup. Flaky third-world countries, empty oil business skyscrapers, bankrupt pie-in-the-sky developments, and leveraged from-here-to-eternity corporate buy-outs have created embarrassingly large bad-loan portfolios. The irony is, these were caused more by ivory tower loaning activities at upper echelons than by peon loan officers at the bottom. But, since manure always flows downhill, repercussions have seeped down to the peon level. Because of screw-ups by top bank management, small business people must deal with loan officers at the bottom who are more conservative than ever.

THE SECOND COMING OF THE WOOLLY MAMMOTH

Besides having to deal with conservatism, there is the problem of technocracy. It used to be that banking was a human activity. The small business person dealt with his or her friendly neighborhood banker.

No more. Friendly Neighborhood Banker now has a partner—Friendly Neighborhood Computer. Banks deal in vast quantities of numbers. What is the stock-in-trade of computers? Crunching vast quantities of numbers. So banks took to computers like nine-year-old kids to Nintendo. They love 'em. It was a marriage made in business heaven.

The first application was accounting. Banks started using computers to keep track of accounts and balances and banking transactions. Then utilization spread to actual operations—cash machines, credit cards, and checkless banking. Now we are at stage three: banks are using computers for analysis and decision making.

In the bank lobby sits your friendly, smiling, hand-shaking banker, "Frank." He looks and acts the same. But, deep down in the bowels of the bank, unseen and unbeknownst to you, lurks "Hal," the bank's computer, complete with blinking lights, whirring disks, and air-conditioned surroundings. Attended to by a team of solicitous computer nerds, like worker termites nudging the pulsating body of the bloated termite queen.

In the good old days, it was Frank you had to get along with for approval of a business loan. Human relationships were the key. You wined and dined Frank and played golf with him (managing to lose on occasion). You joined the same service club and contributed to Frank's favorite charities. You curried Frank's favor because he was your lifeblood, your hidden reserve, your "main man."

Suddenly, Frank seems distant, noncommittal, reserved—more than usual, even for a banker. Maybe even a touch circumspect. It appears Frank doesn't like you anymore. But you are wrong. Of course Frank likes you. It's just that Frank no longer calls the shots. Nowadays, he must reserve judgment on your loan application until he consults with Hal, his microchip-brained guru.

You see, it isn't Frank who analyzes your financial statements; Hal does. Frank doesn't rate your borrowing capacity; that's Hal's job. Frank doesn't make discreet phone calls to check your current credit experience; Hal already has an up-to-date history in his data bank.

THE SECOND COMING OF THE WOOLLY MAMMOTH

Small business banking is a new ball game, kids. Your banker isn't somebody named Frank. Now it's Frank and Hal, or, more properly, Hal and Frank. Small business loan applications these days must pass Hal's gimlet-eyed analysis. Hal is programmed to compute the credit worthiness of small business customers. Say, from zero to 20. If your score is below 10, tough luck, Chuck. Seek a loan elsewhere.

In contrast, pre-Hal banking was subjective. Loan powers resided in the hands of branch bank managers and bank loan officers—not the most obliging of individuals, perhaps, but flesh-and-blood human beings nonetheless, living, breathing, goofing-off, mistake-prone people.

Obtaining a small business loan back then depended upon getting into their good graces. If you bowed and scraped and smooched and schmoozed enough and your finances weren't too far-out ridiculous, chances are they would see their way clear to put some money in your coffers. Then came the advent of the high-tech revolution and shared information, as practiced by Chase Manhattan. At the small business level, we are now looking at program loaning.

The problem is that banks don't really want to loan small businesses money. Put yourself in the banker's boots. Suppose you have $1,000,000 to lend out. Which would you rather do, make one $1,000,000 business loan or one hundred $10,000 business loans? At first impulse, having $1,000,000 spread out over one hundred small loans might seem safer: a not-having-all-your-eggs-in-one-basket sort of thing. Not so. The one big loan is going to be just as safe and probably safer than one hundred small ones. Banks can require 200 percent collateral on loans of any consequence these days. So you can safely bet that the $1,000,000 loan will be well secured.

Secondly, the large loan will be with a bigger business that has superior accounting compared to pee-wee borrowers. Consequently, its financial statements will likely be more accurate and prepared in a more timely manner. As a result, Frank's partner, Hal, has a better chance of keeping track of things. Little guys can more easily conceal problems, whether intentionally or inadvertently. Even if no concealment exists, there is still the perception that *small business* is synonymous with *risky business*.

Finally, it is far cheaper to process and administer one large loan than one hundred small ones. The bank's overhead will be a fraction of what the small ones cost. In short, from their point of view, banks have less risk and more profit on big loans. That is why I say they really don't want to deal with you, the small business peanut account. That is why banks are tight as bark on a tree when considering small business loans. Pawning the decision off onto a computer is a diplomatic way out. Now, of course, banks will officially deny this charge. You will find, however, that the person writing the bank's advertising is not the one who passes out its loan dollars.

How to cope? First of all, the subjective element still does exist. Hal lives mainly in bigger banks. Many smaller banks haven't sold their decision-making soul to the computer yet. Chances are there is a small, locally owned bank in your area still operating under the old scheme of things where loans are based primarily on how its manager sizes you up. Consequently, if you are a little guy, go to a little bank. Seek one without a Hal.

Even in the big banks where Hal has taken over, he can be overridden. Upper-level bank personnel can pull Hal's plug, if they have a mind to. The key is, banks are classic bureaucratic organizations. So, your strategy must focus on traditional bureaucratic weaknesses—rigid hierarchies and cumbersome paperwork. Number one, get acquainted with bankers at as high a bureaucratic level as possible—with someone who has enough authority to override Hal, one hopes. Number two, support your loan application with enormous quantities of paperwork. Give Hal so much information that he gags.

First, let's talk about the hierarchy game. Being a peon account, you will be relegated to a peon loan officer. But sometime or other, you undoubtedly will be introduced to and asked to shake hands with the peon loan officer's boss, or maybe even the boss of bosses. This is merely a courtesy gesture. It is mutually understood that the loan officer's boss won't be the person dealing with your mundane banking affairs. But don't let that stop you from following up with personal contact at the boss level—wining, dining, offering football tickets, whatever you can think of to become personally chummy. And the higher up the bank's organization chart you infiltrate, the better shot you have of getting reasonable treatment from down below. Lower-level bureaucrats not only do their bosses' bidding, they also try to anticipate their bosses' bidding. If the peon loan officer perceives that his or her superiors hold you in high regard, some of that esteem will transfer to his or her relationship with you.

The second part of your strategy is to smother the bank with paperwork. Bureaucrats love files stuffed with documents, so give them what they want. Why are small business people so cloddish in their loan applications? An aura of embarrassment seems to envelop many of them when they set out to borrow money. It appears to be deeply rooted in our culture, as witness the numerous homilies: Who goeth a-borrowing, goeth a-sorrowing; debt is a bottomless sea; the borrower is servant to the lender; debt is the worst poverty. Borrowing has furtive overtones attached to it. For most people it's something they want to get over with as quickly and quietly as possible.

Of course, banks do their part to reinforce such feelings. There must be a special school somewhere that teaches bank loan officers how to transform solid, upstanding citizens into freeloading deadbeats the minute they walk into the bank looking for money. Next to income tax audits, nothing seems more degrading than going hat-in-hand to the bank seeking a loan.

Succumbing to this frame of mind is a mistake. Money is nothing more than a commodity, like pork bellies or molasses. So don't think you are asking for something special when applying for a bank loan. What you are really doing is offering to buy something for a reasonable price— the temporary use of money in exchange for paying the bank interest.

Applying for a loan should be a major production. Don't just go up to the banker and blurt out that you need money. He or she will start asking you questions you aren't prepared to answer. Instead, swamp the banker with details. Enhance your presentation with masses of figures, projections, statistics, rhetoric, and analyses. Even if Hal doesn't like what he sees, a blizzard of paperwork may confuse him. At a minimum, you should furnish the following:

1. Your business's balance sheet, income statement, and cash flow statement—preferably not more than three months old.

2. A cash flow projection (forecast) for the coming year.

3. Your personal net worth statement, also not more than three months old.

4. An aged trial balance of your accounts receivable.

5. A list of major jobs in process and major orders on file.

6. An analysis of what you are going to do with the money and how you plan to pay it back. In other words, a business plan.

The last item mentioned, the business plan, is commonly omitted in small business loan applications. Most people choke up when it comes to writing narrative, so drafting a business plan usually gets ignored. Actually, there isn't that much involved. It's merely a matter of answering seven fundamental questions.

Outline of a Business Plan

The Question	*The Answer*
1. Who am I?	List your internal capabilities: • A history of the firm • Resumes of key employees • Resources of the firm (including advisors) • Significant contracts and agreements • Any competitive advantages you may enjoy
2. Where am I?	Espouse your perception of the external environment: • The market for your products • Pertinent technological developments • The general economic outlook
3. Where am I headed?	Explain your goals: • As to production • As to marketing • As to finances
4. How am I going to get there?	Lay out your organization and management plan: • Your management structure • How you expect to develop an effective labor force • Your administrative and accounting systems and procedures
5. How am I going to make it?	Set forth your production plan: • Basic requirements and procedures • Labor required • Technologies involved • Research and development

6.	How am I going to sell it?	Present your sales and marketing plan: • Your product • Your pricing policy • Your distribution system • Your plans for advertising and promotion
7.	How am I going to pay for it?	Describe your financial plan: • The amount of money you seek • When it is needed and what it is going to be used for • How it will be paid back • Your projected cash flow and financial statements • Major assumptions pertaining to the foregoing

Now, I'm not saying bankers will actually understand all of this. Without Hal's help, most bankers are inept when it comes to financial analysis. They know buzz words and ratios, but never having run a business of their own they don't quite appreciate what it is all about. If you throw enough paperwork at them, though, the volume alone will impress them. Occasionally you may run across a bank that has qualified in-house financial analysts. If this happens, change banks.

The average small business person walks into the bank with a few figures scratched out on the back of an old envelope at the kitchen table instead of a financial plan and comprehensive financial statements. Naturally, the banker gives them a bad time. Meanwhile, all the glib-tongued smoothies with professional applications are walking out with thousands of loan dollars in their pockets. You've got to be more like them.

Let's assume you do survive Hal's scrutiny and ingratiate yourself into the bank's good graces. Here is a rundown of the major types of financing available through banks.

Self-liquidating loans. Banks will loan money for short terms (three months to a year) for a specific purpose that will generate the funds to pay back the loan—in other words, if it is a self-liquidating situation. Seasonal businesses such as fruit packing and toy manufacturing are classic examples. Other examples are manufacturers and contractors needing temporary financing for large jobs. The completion of the job will provide the funds necessary to pay the loan.

Term loans. Banks sometimes make installment loans of one to five years. When they do, they usually tie you into pretty tight knots. You will have to agree to guarantees, pledged assets, restrictions on capital purchases, restrictions on owners' salaries, proof of adequate insurance coverage, and minimum working capital requirements.

Lines of credit. This is an assurance (not a guarantee) that the bank will loan you money up to a predetermined amount when and if you need it. At least once a year, you will be required to "clean out" the line of credit (temporarily reduce the balance to zero).

Receivable loans. Banks will loan money on your receivables, provided they are current. Normally, loans are up to 75 percent of face value. Under this arrangement, you furnish the bank with copies of your customer billings. You are then obliged to turn the collected proceeds over to the bank. A separate so-called "bank control" checking account is often used to handle these transactions.

Flooring. Flooring is similar to borrowing from a pawn shop. Money is loaned on specific inventory items. As the items are sold, their respective flooring loans must be paid off. To make sure borrowers actually pay their flooring, the bank periodically conducts a "flooring check." That is, a bank employee goes to the borrower's store and snoops around the inventory to verify that the merchandise listed on outstanding flooring notes is still physically present (making sure, of course, that the boxes and crates aren't empty). Flooring loans are expensive because of handling and processing costs.

Equipment loans. You can finance equipment purchases through a bank. These are similar to automobile loans. The bank holds a security interest in the equipment as collateral.

Because you are a small operator, the bank isn't going to trust you very far. If you ask for a loan of any consequence, you will have to put up security, such as a blanket lien on inventory and equipment, or a second mortgage on real estate. If you have marketable investments, such as stocks or bonds, the bank may hold them as collateral. If your business operates as a corporation, you undoubtedly will be required to personally guarantee its loans.

Bank money is basically short-term money. That is, you have to keep it revolving and pay it back in a year or two. And it is costly. One way or another, the bank is going to nick you for double digit interest. But there isn't much choice. Nobody accumulates enough to completely finance his or her own business. Eventually we must all visit our "friendly" neighborhood banker and partner Hal. So make your peace with them at the start. The devil of finance and the devil's machine must have their due.

CHAPTER 27

ACCOUNTING FOR

NON-ACCOUNTANTS

Money is like manure, not good unless it is spread around.   Francis Bacon

I could teach you a lot about accounting. But I won't. It would bore you to sleep. Accounting is chalk-dry stuff. After a minute or so, your eyelids would droop. Not to mention, it would take considerable time and many pages to impart anything meaningful, and this book is supposed to be reasonably short. (Lengthy ones don't sell very well, you know.)

Besides, you're better off having your book work done by a hired accountant. Spend your time learning how to make money rather than how to count it. However, there are a few things about accounting you should know if you are going to be a successful entrepreneur. To begin with, most small businesses have a tough time coming up with accurate financial statements. The primary reason for this is that small firms can't afford the in-house accounting skills they really need. In addition, their paperwork is usually sloppy. The combination results in take-them-with-a-grain-of-salt financial statements.

The idea of financial statements is to match income with the particular expenses incurred creating that income. The difference between the two is your net profit. So what happens if inept accounting causes expenses to be recorded in the wrong month? Suppose you sold a truckload of

Whoozits in January but paid for them in February. If you don't go back and record the February payment as a January account payable, you will show a big profit in January and a big loss in February and be thoroughly confused. Plus, your banker will think you don't know what you are doing.

Or, suppose a customer buys some Whoozits in January but doesn't pick them up until February. Then suppose you mistakenly include them in your January 31 Whoozit inventory count because they sat on your factory floor that date. You will have recorded the sale in January but not the cost of the sale. Income and expense will be mismatched, and your profit and loss statements (P&Ls) will look goofy.

Accountants call this a "cut-off" problem. The reason cut-off mistakes happen so often in small business is that there's generally some poorly trained individual doing the bookkeeping. Untrained people trying to fill an accountant's role have difficulty comprehending the cut-off concept. The problem is especially acute in manufacturing and construction where there are inventories and work-in-process to deal with.

Another reason small business financial statements are hard to do is that misclassifications are common. I guarantee that when you've got amateurs doing your books, they will classify things wrong. Like putting the cost of a new machine into "shop expense" instead of capitalizing it as a "fixed asset." Or charging withheld payroll taxes to "taxes" rather than "wages." On top of this, small business source documents are characteristically prepared in a more cavalier manner, which makes it extra hard to account for them.

Sounds hopeless, doesn't it? What's a small business person to do, accounting-wise? This is a serious question, folks, because lack of adequate accounting records is one of the most common factors found in small business failures. All too often entrepreneurs discover too late that they are running on empty. Poor accounting records cause them to operate in the dark, so they discover too late that they are slipping over the edge of a financial precipice.

The thing to keep in mind is this: Don't even try to run your business with financial statements! Mind you, I didn't say that you shouldn't prepare them. I only said you shouldn't run your business with them. Besides lacking accuracy, small business financial statements are a rearview mirror. They're history. They record things happening many months ago. They're Monday morning quarterbacking. They're a phone call to the doctor after the patient is dead.

Instead, you should try to operate by looking ahead. Project with *budgeted* figures what you think or expect is going to happen. Only after the budget-making process is finished should you take into account the history that financial statements portray. Coming along after the fact, financial statements will show where you went wrong in anticipating results. Then you can revise future actions accordingly.

Most small business people plod along day to day focusing on what's bugging them at the moment. By the time their financials are prepared, a whole new swarm of problems and concerns is bedeviling them. In contrast, operating by budget gives them the chance to think prospectively, to get ahead of the game rather than play catch-up.

Remember the prior pontifications regarding goal setting? Budgets are a practical application. Budgets portray what your financial statements will look like if you achieve what you intend to accomplish in the next accounting period. The gimmick is, a budget forces you to utilize goals because it involves analyzing, anticipating, and estimating. The mental exercise of preparing a budget is what is important, because it entails goal setting. The figures themselves are merely by-products.

Suppose your budget predicts sales of $200,000 for the quarter. Then you calculate expenses to be $210,000. You are staring an ugly $10,000 loss in the face. Guess what happens? You will automatically try to figure ways and means of forestalling that loss. But you will be doing this ahead of time, before the loss actually happens. You will be planning specific actions aimed at eliminating a loss for the quarter. On the other hand, waiting for financial statements to arrive before recognizing the situation means the loss has already occurred and you are probably well on your way to piling up another for the current accounting period, as well.

So, the real value of financial statements isn't in portraying whether you made any money. Their usefulness is in showing you why the amount you thought you were going to make turns out different. If you know where and why your old budget was off target, won't that help you be more accurate when calculating the next budget? Of course it will. And if you are more accurate the next time around, won't that help you take action sooner to improve your profitability? For sure it will. A guided missile arrives on target by perceiving where it is going rather than where it has been.

"But you just got through telling us that small business financial statements are garbage," you might ask. "How can we use them for this or any other purpose if they contain accounting mistakes?"

I didn't say small business financial statements are garbage; I just said that many of them contain inaccuracies. But that doesn't mean they are completely useless. The thing to keep in mind is the art of compromise. A partial answer is better than no answer, 75 percent accuracy is better than random numbers, and an incomplete accounting system is better than no system at all.

The reason you can satisfactorily function with semiaccurate accounting is that, to a certain extent, it is feasible for small business people to run by the seat of their pants. The limited scope of their operations causes most small businesses to wind up being managed essentially *ad hoc*. Owners typically become so familiar with the details of their operations that they don't need exact figures to know whether they are making money.

Of course, seat of the pants management can be deceptive. It's a wise seat of the pants operator who knows the true costs of his or her business. That is why financial statements are important—to confirm or deny the owner's ongoing perceptions and assumptions and to destroy erroneous myths. But financial statements don't have to be completely accurate in accordance with academic standards to accomplish this objective. Because of the average owner's familiarity with his or her business, 100 percent accuracy isn't necessary to know what is going on.

By the way, an excessively elaborate accounting system is just as big a mistake as inadequate accounting. Accounting systems that are too complicated invariably break down, and all the paperwork created becomes a muddled mess. This, again, causes a small business person to wind up flying blind.

Here is a practical accounting shortcut that is enormously helpful. It avoids complications but at the same time gives essential information. Figure out the following three items:

1. Your daily sales

2. Your percentage of gross profit

3. Your average daily overhead expense

Once you have a reasonably accurate idea of what these are, you can pretty much tell on a daily basis whether you are making any money.

Suppose your average gross profit is 40 cents on a dollar's worth of sales—in other words, 40 percent. And suppose your overhead expense averages $1,000 every day you are open for business. (Overhead consists of expenses that are relatively constant and don't vary much with sales, such as office salaries, rent, utilities, insurance, office expenses, and depreciation.) Your high school algebra should tell you that $2,500 of sales are needed every day to break even.

> sales × .40 = $1,000 of overhead, or
> sales = $1,000/.40 = $2,500

If today's sales equal $2,500, you broke even. If sales were more than that, you made money; if they were less, you'd better start a full court press.

The point is, the only figure you have to track during the month is daily sales. The beauty of this is you know immediately how you are doing. You don't have to wait until you are 10 miles downstream to find out how fast you were going upstream. You have instant feedback, which is a very powerful tool. When your financial statements finally do arrive, you can verify that, yes, your sales margin was 40 percent and that, yes, your overhead did, in fact, amount to $1,000 per day.

Obviously, if significant variations show up from those figures, you will try to figure out why. But look what happens when you do that. You are using accounting figures and are analyzing costs. You have become a financial analyst! (Wouldn't your mother be proud of you now?)

So, be sure to *have* an accounting system in your business, but use it properly, as a check against previously calculated budgets. Also, for gawd's sake, keep it simple. Installing a sophisticated accounting system in a small business is like turning a B-1 bomber over to a tribe of primitive savages. That airplane won't fly without qualified pilots and mechanics to go along with it. Neither will a sophisticated accounting system work without qualified accountants and bookkeepers to work it.

I once knew a little company in the embroidery business that had a wonderfully complex computerized accounting system, including a pricing system for determining how much to charge customers. The computer calculated the price charged for a job by multiplying standardized variable cost rates and fixed cost rates by the number of stitches involved in an embroidery job. It looked beautifully impressive and authoritative when you called up the program on screen.

The trouble was, nobody had enough accounting expertise to go back and figure out whether the cost standards used for pricing were realistic in relation to actual costs. The fact is, they weren't. Furthermore, the accounting system was so complex, the financial statements were six to nine months late and usually were wrong at that. The company lost money hand over fist, but its owners couldn't figure out why, because they had so many customers and were so busy! Who wouldn't be busy doing work below cost?

Of course they went bust. Their system was gorgeous from an accountant's point of view. But, from a practical standpoint, it was worse than useless. It not only failed to provide accurate information, it lulled them into self-deception by making them think they had a modern, up-to-date, state-of-the-art system.

They did. But it wasn't functioning. I don't care how good your system is; it cannot—I repeat, cannot—spit out good figures if it's operated by primitive accountants. The company's accounting system exceeded the capabilities of its personnel.

The moral is, if you are going to spend money on an accounting system, the area to splurge on is in hiring personnel. I don't care how good your system is on paper; if airheads are running it, you're bound to have a mess on your hands. And don't think having the latest computer will solve everything. Small business neophytes are easily seduced by the word *computer.* They automatically genuflect whenever the word is mentioned. What they don't realize is that computers involve much more than hardware and software. You also need "peopleware." In the last analysis, "peopleware" is the most important element of any computerized accounting system.

Here are some hints to keep in mind when planning and using your bookkeeping system.

- The main thing is to leave plenty of tracks. Have everything written down in some kind of logical, systematic manner.

- Use checks instead of cash for every expense you can. Canceled checks and bank statements are excellent records.

- Deposit *all* receipts in the bank. If you keep cash in your pocket for payment of expenses, you'll likely lose track of what your real expenses were.

- Use credit cards for travel and entertainment expenses. The IRS is extraordinarily picky about supporting documentation for travel and entertainment expenses. With a credit card, at least you have proof of the time, amount, and place. You can probably recall from your appointment calendar who the money was spent on and why.

- Regardless what kind of bookkeeping system you use, be it hand-posted, computer, or one-write, be sure to create "control totals" so you can verify that individual postings are correct. In other words, accumulate the total amounts posted to receivables and payables so you have a balancing figure against which you can check the sum of the individual accounts.

- If your business involves inventories, count and price them at least twice a year. This is known as taking a physical inventory. Physical inventories are necessary for accurate financial statements. Without a physical count, the profit on your books is nothing more than an estimate.

- Pay creditors based upon original invoices rather than monthly statements. It's usually difficult to reconcile purchases with suppliers' statements because of different posting date cut-offs. If you base payments on original invoices rather than on statements, you can't go wrong.

- After you pay an invoice, write *paid* on your file copy. Also, jot down the date and check number. This eliminates the possibility of paying or processing the same invoice twice.

- Check the product, prices, and quantities on your bills—if not for every item, then at least on a test basis or on major dollar items. Everyone makes mistakes, and, in the case of vendors, the mistakes are often in their favor. The time and bother involved in checking their invoices pays off.

- Get professional help from an outside accountant before setting up your bookkeeping and accounting system.

- Don't be a basket case. Don't take a bunch of mixed-up receipts and papers to your accountant at the end of the year and expect him or her to make figures materialize by waving a magic wand over the mess.

Accountant Street Gangs   Gary Larson

CHAPTER 28

DECIPHERING THE SACRED TABLETS

It is likewise to be observed that this society hath a peculiar chant and jargon of their own, that no other mortal can understand, and wherein all their laws are written, which they take special care to multiply.
Jonathan Swift

As previously indicated, I have no more hope of turning you into an accountant than I do of changing you into a frog. But perhaps I can give you a basic understanding of accountants' work products. Even bankers and experienced business people have trouble understanding financial statements. They contain just enough jargon to be confusing. Here is a rundown of their more commonly used terms (rivit, rivit).

Current Assets These are assets that can or will be turned into cash before the year is over. In other words, assets that are "liquid," such as accounts receivable, inventories, prepaid expenses, marketable securities, and, of course, cash itself.

Fixed Assets These are assets that will last physically more than one year, such as buildings, land, equipment, and vehicles. CPAs often use the term *plant, property, and equipment* instead of *fixed assets* because they think it's more descriptive.

Intangible Assets These are fixed assets you can't touch, see, or smell. In other words, they are intangible. Usually a piece of paper evidences their existence. Some examples are the costs of obtaining a patent, costs of organizing a corporation, costs of a noncompetition agreement, and the cost of buying goodwill.

Accumulated Depreciation This is the amount of fixed assets you've written off as an expense due to wear, tear, and obsolescence. Depreciation is something you claim when you file your tax return but not when you talk to a potential buyer.

Amortization This is the same thing as depreciation, except that it applies to intangible assets. Don't ask me why it isn't also called depreciation.

Allowance for Doubtful Accounts This is the amount of money owed by deadbeats whom you suspect aren't going to pay up. However, you still have some forlorn hope they will, so you leave the amount they owe on the books with an off-setting loss reserve account.

Fifo Inventory *Fifo* stands for "first in, first out." Fifo accounts for inventory by assuming it consists of the items last purchased. It assumes you sell your oldest inventory first, which is smart merchandising.

Lifo Inventory *Lifo* stands for "last in, first out." It is the opposite of fifo. It assumes you have the same goods in inventory you started out with years ago. In other words, that your most recent acquisitions are what you sell first. Naturally, you hope this doesn't actually happen, but it is a good assumption to make for tax purposes. During times of inflation, valuing your inventory at old costs reduces taxable income.

Prepaid Expenses   These are the expenses you've paid for but haven't consumed—like next month's rent paid in advance, office supplies that will last a year, or insurance premiums that cover the next nine months.

Current Liabilities   These include all liabilities that must be paid within one year—accounts payable, short-term bank notes, accrued expenses, one year's worth of mortgage payments, and so on.

Accrued Liabilities   These include money you owe but haven't received a bill for. Some examples are utility costs, property taxes, income tax withheld on salaries, and accumulated interest on promissory notes. You might like to forget about them but know they won't forget about you, so you face the music and accrue them while waiting for the actual billing to arrive.

Long-Term Liabilities   This category consists of debts due beyond one year. These are primarily mortgage and contract payments.

Contingent Liabilities   These are obligations you may get stuck with but only if you're unlucky. An example is your brother-in-law's bank loan you co-signed in a weak moment and kicked yourself for later. Liability is contingent upon whether or not he lives up to your suspicions of being a deadbeat.

Working Capital   This is the difference between current assets and current liabilities. It is the amount of cash you would have if your inventory were sold, accounts receivable were received, and all current bills were paid. Working capital is something it is nice to have lots of.

Deferred Credits   This represents the income you've received but haven't earned yet, such as being paid in advance for services to be performed later, which, by the way, is very poor policy if you are the customer.

THE SECOND COMING OF THE WOOLLY MAMMOTH

Paid-in Capital This is the amount stockholders invest in the corporation over and above the par value of their capital stock.

Retained Earnings These are the profits a corporation has earned over the years not distributed to stockholders as dividends.

Stockholders' Equity This is the net worth of a corporation, assuming everything is worth the figures shown on the balance sheet. Basically, it includes what stockholders originally put into the corporation plus retained earnings.

Cost of Goods Sold This represents the direct costs of producing or acquiring whatever it is you sell: materials, if you are a retailer; materials and labor, if you are a contractor; materials, labor, and factory overhead, if you are a manufacturer.

Net Income This is what comes out of the spigot after dumping all income, revenues, gains, expenses, costs, and losses into one giant pot.

Cash Basis Accounting This means that you will be recording income only when the cash is actually received and expenses only after the checks are written. This is a simplified method of accounting generally frowned upon except for extremely small businesses.

Accrual Basis Accounting This means recording income and expenses based upon when the deal is struck rather than when cash is exchanged. This method takes receivables and payables into account when calculating profits.

As you can see, it is simpler to use accounting terms than to write the associated definitions. Accounting terminology is a form of shorthand. You have to live with it a while before it connotes real meaning.

Once you get used to the special language and format, financial statements aren't that hard to understand. Here is one for the Doozy Company, simplified and boiled down to its essentials:

The Doozy Company
Income Statement

Sales	$750,000
Cost of Sales	450,000
Gross Profit	300,000

Overhead Expenses

Office and sales salaries	102,000
Truck expense	38,000
Owner's salary	35,000
Bad debts	30,000
Taxes	19,000
Utilities and maintenance	16,000
Office expense	15,000
Depreciation	11,000
Interest expense	10,000
	276,000

Net Income Before Income Tax	24,000
Income Tax	4,000
Net Income	20,000
Retained Earnings at Beginning of Year	75,000
Retained Earnings at End of Year	$ 95,000

The Doozy Company
Balance Sheet

Assets

Current Assets

Cash	$ 5,000
Receivables	180,000
Inventory	15,000
	200,000

Fixed Assets

Buildings and equipment	200,000
Less accumulated depreciation	(55,000)
	145,000
	$345,000

Liabilities and Stockholders' Equity

Current Liabilities

Accounts payable	$ 75,000
Bank note	25,000
Current portion of L.T. debt	25,000
	125,000

Long-Term Liabilities

Building and equipment mortgages	75,000
Total liabilities	$200,000

Stockholders' Equity

Capital stock	50,000
Retained earnings	95,000
	145,000
	$345,000

First of all, notice there are two parts to Doozy's financial statements:

1. The income statement, which tells you how much Doozy made.

2. The balance sheet, which tells you how much Doozy's got left.

Income statements show the amount of money you made (or lost) between two points in time. Balance sheets portray your assets, liabilities, and net worth at the end of that particular time.

Once financial statements have been prepared, it is important to know how to use them. Utilizing financial statements is a four-step process:

1. First, try to figure out what happened.

2. Next, figure out what did or didn't happen that you thought was going to happen.

3. Then figure out why it did or didn't happen.

4. Finally, figure out what, if anything, to do about it.

To accomplish these things, you need the budget discussed in the previous chapter. Plus, you need some basis of comparison, and you need to know the relationships between accounts. For comparisons, the thing to do is line up last year's figures beside this year's. To establish relationships between expenses and sales, compute their percentages on the income statement. Doing these things to Doozy's financial statements makes them look like the statements below. (Stay with me, now! Don't freak out yet. These statements may look complicated because of the additional figures portrayed, but they aren't as bad as they first appear.)

THE SECOND COMING OF THE WOOLLY MAMMOTH

The Doozy Company
Comparative Income Statement
(In thousands of dollars)

	Actual				Budget	
	This Year		Last Year			
Sales	$750	100%	$655	100%	$700	100%
Cost of Sales	450	60	360	55	385	55
Gross Profit	300	40	295	45	315	45
Overhead Expenses						
Office and sales salaries	102	14	100	14	105	15
Truck expense	38	5	40	6	42	6
Owner's salary	35	5	35	7	35	5
Bad debts	30	4	15	2	15	2
Taxes	19	3	17	3	18	3
Utilities and maintenance	16	2	14	2	15	2
Office expense	15	2	16	2	20	3
Depreciation	11	1	11	2	9	1
Interest expense	10	1	12	2	9	1
	276	37	260	40	268	38
Net Income Before Tax	24	3	35	5	47	7
Income Tax	4	–	5	–	7	1
Net Income	20	3%	30	5%	40	6%
Beg. Retained Earnings	75		45		75	
End. Retained Earnings	$ 95		$ 75		$115	

THE SECOND COMING OF THE WOOLLY MAMMOTH

The Doozy Company
Comparative Balance Sheet
(In thousands of dollars)

| | Actual | | | |
	This Year	Last Year	+ (−)	Budget
Current Assets				
Cash..................................	$ 5	$ 15	$(10)	$ 25
Receivables	180	100	80	110
Inventory	15	10	5	20
	200	125	75	155
Fixed Assets				
Building and equipment.......................	200	194	6	194
Less accumulated depreciation	(55)	(44)	(11)	(53)
	145	150	(5)	141
	$ 345	$ 275	$ 70	$ 296
Current Liabilities				
Accounts payable....................	$ 75	$ 30	$ 45	$ 35
Bank notes..........................	25	5	20	–
Current portion of L. T. debt.........	25	27	(2)	25
	125	62	63	60
Long-Term Liabilities				
Building and equipment mortgages...	75	88	(13)	72
Total liabilities	200	150	50	132
Stockholders' Equity				
Capital stock	50	50	–	50
Retained earnings	95	75	20	115
	145	125	20	165
	$ 345	$ 275	$ 70	$ 297

As you can see, these statements give us much more to work with. Now, how is Mr. Doozy's company doing, and where can it stand improvement?

Well, first of all, this year's profit is $20,000. That amounts to only three percent of sales. Sounds like a pretty thin profit margin, doesn't it? But this isn't the percentage calculation that is important.

What counts is the percent of profit Doozy made on the dollars invested in his business. In other words, what was Doozy's rate of return? Doozy's average stockholder's equity was $135,000: ($145,000 + $125,000) × (1/2) = $135,000. On that amount of investment, he earned a profit of $20,000. This means he had a 15 percent return on his money: ($20,000/$135,000 = .148). That's pretty good, although, considering the risks involved in running a small business, it's nothing to write home about.

This year's net income, though, is $20,000 less than the $40,000 profit his budget projected and $10,000 less than last year's profit, which was $30,000. This should raise Doozy's eyebrows, because his sales were actually more than projected. His budget anticipated $700,000, but actual sales amounted to $750,000. Yet, profits dropped. This is bad. Very, very bad. What caused decreased profits on increased sales?

For one thing, cost of sales jumped from 55 percent of sales to 60 percent. If cost of sales had stayed at the budgeted 55 percent, Doozy would have another $37,000 of profit and would have beaten his budget. What happened? There are a number of possibilities. Doozy may have incurred higher costs for wages and materials. If that is the case, he should have raised his prices—either that or gone out and found cheaper labor and less expensive materials. On the other hand, Doozy's plant operations may have become less efficient. His productivity may have dropped. If so, he had better hustle his buns out into the plant to try to discover what is going on. Another possibility is that competition may have forced him to cut prices, thereby reducing profit margins. Exactly what did happen is up to Doozy to find out. The point is, his financials spotlight the fact that his gross profit margins are less than expected.

We also see that overhead expenses increased $16,000 over last year and were $8,000 more than budget. Percentage-wise, though, overhead dropped in relation to sales (37 percent vs. 40 percent), so the dollar increase in overhead doesn't seem out of line. Overhead expenses shouldn't vary much with sales. Ideally, they should remain relatively constant in terms of total dollars from one period to another, because they relate more to the fact of being in business than to the amount of product produced or sold.

In looking over specific overhead items, however, we see that bad debts are four percent of sales. That is a high percentage, much higher than his budget had projected. It is even higher than Doozy's net profit margin. The dramatic increase in sales must have included flaky customers. Doozy had better tighten up his credit and collection procedures.

Bankers are obsessed with what is called the *current asset ratio*. This is the ratio between current assets (assets that will be turned into cash within one year) and current liabilities (liabilities due to be paid within one year). If your current asset ratio is two to one or more, your banker will love you and might even pick up the tab at lunch. If it gets down to one to one, you've got major problems, and your banker will probably forget your name. Doozy's current assets are $200,000 (cash, receivables, and inventory). Current liabilities are $125,000 (accounts payable and bank note). That is a 1.6-to-one ratio, which is respectable. However, last year's current asset ratio was two to one. If Doozy's current ratio keeps declining at this same rate, he soon won't be able to afford his own lunch, let alone the banker's. It is apparent Doozy has too much money tied up in receivables. His customers owe him $180,000, which equals 62 days of sales.

$$\frac{\$750,000 \text{ annual sales}}{260 \text{ annual business days}} = \$2,885 \text{ sales per day}$$

$$\frac{\$180,000 \text{ accounts receivable}}{\$2,885 \text{ sales per day}} = \begin{array}{l}62 \text{ days of sales in} \\ \text{accounts receivable}\end{array}$$

If Doozy had kept receivables to last year's level, which was 40 days of sales, he would have $65,000 less in receivables and $65,000 more cash. That would have reduced his payables, thereby making his current asset ratio the magic two to one. What with both a high bad debt ratio and a high level of receivables, it is clear Doozy is soft on collections. Either that, or he is making sales without checking the credit of his customers.

THE SECOND COMING OF THE WOOLLY MAMMOTH

Now, back up a minute. Remember where we figured the rate of return on Doozy's investment? It was:

$$\frac{\$20,000 \text{ profit}}{\$135,000 \text{ average net worth}} = 15 \text{ percent}$$

That was an important calculation. Return on your investment, after all, is what it is all about. Large, publicly held corporations try like mad to increase their earnings per share of stock every year. Paradoxically, small business people hardly ever think in those terms. They focus on the dollar amount of profit rather than on the rate of return made on their investment.

However, the way we calculated Doozy's return was misleading. We assumed the figures on Doozy's books represent true values. That is hardly ever the case. Accounting statements are the product of accounting rules and conventions applied to historic costs. The results may or may not reflect the true economic state of affairs. It has been said that accountants and economists mine the same materials, but out of them, they fashion remarkably different products.

Doozy's building and equipment show up on his books as $145,000. But that is not what they are really worth. Book figures merely represent the original cost of assets less whatever depreciation has been written off to expense.

Depreciation is an arbitrary figure. It seldom, if ever, represents true economic expense—especially real estate. Inflation, expanding population, and shrinking resources usually cause real estate to appreciate rather than depreciate. Equipment, on the other hand, often depreciates faster than book figures. Here are the actual market values of Doozy's fixed assets compared with book value.

THE SECOND COMING OF THE WOOLLY MAMMOTH

	Original Cost	Less Accumulated Depreciation	Book Value	Actual Values
Buildings and land	$150,000	$ (30,000)	$120,000	$220,000
Equipment	50,000	(25,000)	25,000	10,000
	$200,000	$ (55,000)	$145,000	$230,000

See? I told you so. Doozy's fixed assets are worth $85,000 more than what his balance sheet shows, which means his net worth is $85,000 greater in real economic terms. The fair market value (FMV) of Doozy's average net worth is $220,000, not $135,000. Therefore, his real rate of return is:

$$\frac{\$20,000 \text{ profit}}{\$220,000 \text{ FMV of average net worth}} = 9 \text{ percent}$$

Based upon the real worth of Doozy's assets, he only made nine percent instead of 15 percent. He could do as well if he sold his business and invested the proceeds in a long-term CD.

What I'm trying to illustrate here is that you can't necessarily take financial statements at their face value. They may contain hidden assets, as in Doozy's case. Or, conversely, assets may be overstated. Accounts receivable may include unrecognized bad debts. Inventories may be inaccurate. Big bills may be omitted from accounts payable. The small business owner may have personal assets buried in his or her balance sheet. A personal boat and camper may be included in "equipment." The company may be paying some of the owner's personal living expenses and calling it overhead. He or she may be renting a building to the corporation at an unrealistic rental rate. All sorts of distortions and inaccuracies are possible. This is particularly so in small business, where controls and accounting talent are normally weak.

If you are serious about analyzing financial statements, you must be aware of these things. One device used to make financial statements more accurate is to have them audited. In this procedure, an outside CPA performs certain elaborate audit steps designed to ensure the correctness of the final figures. Audits, however, are horrendously expensive. For this reason, small businesses rarely have them done, which is why the qualifying phrase *reviewed* (or *compiled) without audit* accompanies most small business financial statements.

Reviewed (or *compiled) without audit* means the CPA did not perform the audit steps necessary to be able to certify as a professional that the financial statements reasonably represent the business's financial position in accordance with generally accepted accounting principles (commonly referred to by the buzz word *GAAP*). In other words, what you see may or may not be what you get; so don't sue me, the accountant, if things turn out different.

The Securities and Exchange Commission requires all publicly held corporations to be audited. Small businesses, though, are audited only on special occasions because of the high costs involved. Banks and bonding companies sometimes require audits before they will loan or bond a business. Sometimes audits are performed when a business is being sold. Usually, though, owners themselves must check their statements for accuracy.

Half of the time, when I show business owners a profitable financial statement, they say something like, "Whadd'ya mean I made $20,000? If I made that much money, where is it? I haven't any more in the bank today than I had last year."

As a matter of fact, Mr. Doozy is pointing that out to us this very moment. We claim he made $20,000. "But," says he, "I have $10,000 less cash today than I had last year. How come? You must have made a mistake."

Unless profit turns up as cash in the till, many people have trouble believing it exists. To solve conceptual problems like this, a third form of financial statement needs to be created. It is called a cash flow statement. CPA-prepared financial statements nearly always include a cash flow statement. Unfortunately, small business people often skip a cash flow statement when they prepare financial statements internally.

THE SECOND COMING OF THE WOOLLY MAMMOTH

Income statements, remember, tell you how much you made, and balance sheets tell you how much you've got left. Well, cash flow statements explain what you did with it. Here is a cash flow statement for Doozy Company.

The Doozy Company
Cash Flow Statement

Cash Flow from Operations
    Net income, accrual basis $20,000
    Adjustments for non-cash transactions
        Depreciation........................... 11,000
        Increase in accounts receivable .... (80,000)
        Increase in inventory .... (5,000)
        Increase in accounts payable 45,000
        Increase in bank notes 20,000
        Decrease in current portion of L.T. debt... (2,000)
            Cash basis income..................... 9,000

Cash Flow from Long-Term Financing
    Principal payments on mortgages........... (13,000)

Cash Flow from Long-Term Investments
    Purchase of equipment..................... (6,000)

Net Cash Flow for the Year .... (10,000)

Beginning Cash.............................. 15,000

Ending Cash .... $ 5,000

In other words, Doozy's operations made $20,000 of profit on an accrual basis but only cranked out $9,000 on a cash basis, chiefly because of the big "blip" in accounts receivable. He used $13,000 for mortgage payments and paid $6,000 for new equipment. As a result, he wound up with $10,000 less cash for the year.

THE SECOND COMING OF THE WOOLLY MAMMOTH

Responding to Doozy's question, we can now explain that his profit is tied up in new equipment, more receivables, and increased equity in fixed assets. Presumably, this makes him feel better and he will now, with no further reluctance, pay us our accounting fee. Cash flow statements can be very illuminating and ought to be prepared more often.

Generally speaking, that is how you go about analyzing financial statements. They should be used as tools for making management decisions regarding future operations. All too often, financial statements are meaningful only to the accountant who prepared them. The small business owner merely looks at the bottom line, grunts, and continues with what he or she was doing before the statements were handed over. I strongly advise learning how to understand and analyze financial statements. The insights to be gained will surprise you. Trust me.

CHAPTER 29

THE ONE-MINUTE

COST ACCOUNTANT*

*(Warning: Skipping this chapter
could be bad for your financial health.)*

Financial statements are the forest; cost accounts are the trees. That is what cost accounting is all about: measuring the individual sticks that make up the forest.

Cost accounting is often the most neglected aspect of small business accounting. This is ironic, because cost accounting is vital for intelligent management of a business. The fact that your financial statements show that you broke even last year is interesting and important information. But what does it really tell you in terms of what needs to be done to pump up profits?

Perhaps you made money on gidgets but lost money producing widgets. Widget manufacturing costs may have increased significantly since the last time they were priced out. Perhaps marketing and distribution costs destroyed their gross profit margin. Maybe too much overhead is involved in making widgets. Good cost accounting gives you this information, whereas general financial statements leave you clueless.

Conversely, if you realized just how profitable the gidget line was, you

*This chapter is adapted from an article, "Cost Accounting: Shows What's Profitable— and What's Not," *D&B Reports* (January 1987).

would undoubtedly channel more sales effort their way. Gidgets may be a neglected marketing stepchild simply because you have no appreciation for the magnitude of their contribution to profits. Without knowing how much profit potential they contain, management must rely on intuition and "guesstimates" and may easily overemphasize the wrong activities. We are right back to what was described in Chapter 27—using financial statements to correct misbegotten preconceptions, only now we are taking it a step further by analyzing the company's parts rather than the company as a whole.

By comparing cost accounting details with previous estimates of production costs, insights may come to light that otherwise would lay submerged in the lump-sum figures of the income statement. Okay, the financial statements show big cost variances from budget. But where exactly are the overruns being created? Cost accounting pinpoints the location.

Pretend you are a small general contractor and have two jobs going. One involves constructing a duplex. The other is a remodel job of a small office building. Suppose, further, your financial statements show the following:

Condensed Income Statement

Gross revenues from jobs in progress	$300,000
Labor costs	(100,000)
Materials and other job costs	(150,000)
Overhead expenses	(30,000)
Net income	$ 20,000

Now, it would be nice to know how much of your $20,000 profit is attributable to each job, wouldn't it? Suppose you are making all of your profit on the remodel and losing money on the duplex? If you knew this, you might be able to turn the duplex job around by kicking the job foreman's butt. In addition, you would probably alter your cost estimates the next time a similar job came up for bid. That is what cost accounting is all about. You can't tell the players without a program.

Cost accounting is simple in theory. All you do is classify individual costs into subcategories instead of just one expense account. For example, an invoice from Ajax Lumber Company for $1,000 might be classified as: *Materials, $1,000; Job #101*. Total materials for the month are then subtotaled by individual job numbers. The same is done with labor and supplies.

Costs can be broken down even further. A construction company payroll check might be classified this way:

Primary classification:	Labor
Secondary classification:	Job number
Tertiary classification:	Foundation work
Quaternary classification:	Excavation

Multifield numbering systems are used to achieve the detail breakdowns. For instance, the first three digits of the numbering system indicate the general ledger account number.

Example: 500 = direct labor (Primary classification)

The next three digits indicate the number assigned to that particular job.

Example: 101 = the job name (Secondary classification)

The next two digits indicate the cost category within the job.

Example: 11 = foundation work (Tertiary classification)

Finally, two more digits indicate the subcategory within the cost category.

Example: 15 = excavation (Quaternary classification)

Thus, the following number is assigned to that particular payroll check: 500-101-11-15.

It looks a little like a zip code, doesn't it? Of course it does, because the same principle is involved. The objective is to collect and summarize the various cost accounting breakdowns and mail them to their associated revenue categories.

Tracking that much detail is an awesome chore. With manual bookkeeping systems, it involves armies of bookkeepers and an atrocious amount of time. No wonder small businesses traditionally shy away from cost accounting.

Then came the revolution: cheap computers and inexpensive software. Today, sophisticated cost accounting is feasible even for small businesses. Yet, they have been slow to implement the new technology. The problem is, more than computers are needed. Skilled accountants are required to assign cost codes to source documents in a reliable manner. But it gets worse. It is not simply a matter of jotting down code numbers on payroll checks and material invoices. Those costs are easy to classify because they are usually direct in nature. Typically, a close link exists between production materials and labor and a specific revenue activity. Unfortunately, many costs are not so directly related.

How do you allocate insurance or rent or supplies or advertising to the products being produced? What about the expense of repairing machinery, or utility costs? Overhead items like these result from the general fact of being in business rather than as a direct function of cranking out specific products. Logical, rational methods for allocating overhead costs must be established to complete the cost-accounting picture. This takes subjective judgment.

Cost accounting is not a matter of sorting a bunch of marbles by their colors. Many costs can't be allocated one at a time in elemental form. Instead, they must be stuffed together into so-called "cost accounting pools" according to some logical basis for homogeneity. The total costs in cost pools are then spread out among jobs or units of production or departments based upon some sort of rational criteria.

This is when people who have companies with small accounting resources start to drop out. They roll their eyes and say, "Those are fine concepts to talk about, Mr. CPA, but I've got a bunch of orders to get out the door." Not to worry. In small business, you don't need the same accounting sophistication as General Motors or IBM. As Professor Ronald Gist of the University of Denver says, "Nobody can afford the cost of perfect information." As "Perfesser" Frost says, "Some information is better than no information, and 75 percent accuracy is better than no accuracy at all."

Even if you ignore overhead items and allocate only direct labor and direct materials, that is still superior to no cost accounting whatsoever.

This is called *direct costing*. Although it is primitive in terms of cost accounting concepts, it still provides vital information, because direct costs are usually the major expense in many commercial activities. And direct costs normally can be tracked in a fairly straightforward manner.

Going beyond direct costing, most small businesses need at most only three overhead pools. Classifying overhead expense into the following three categories will generate significant cost/production relationships:

Factory Overhead = Indirect labor, power, factory maintenance, supervision, depreciation, and so forth

Selling and Marketing = Sales commissions, advertising, travel, trade shows, shipping, and so on

General and Administrative = Office expense, telephone, office salaries, supplies, insurance, business taxes, and whatever

The next step is to determine how those cost pools should be allocated to specific jobs or products. The most common allocation methods are: (1) direct labor dollars, (2) direct labor hours, (3) direct material costs, (4) machine hours, or (5) some combination of these factors.

Direct labor dollars is usually the easiest allocation base to implement. It works this way:

Step 1: $\dfrac{\text{(factory overhead costs)}}{\text{(total direct labor costs)}}$ = (factory overhead rate)

Step 2: (factory overhead rate) × (widget direct labor costs)
= (amount of factory overhead allocated to widgets)

The same exercise can be performed on cost pools for selling and marketing and for general and administrative. The costs dumped into these pools are divided by total company-wide direct labor costs, creating overhead rates. These rates are multiplied by the direct labor incurred producing widgets. The result is the total cost of producing widgets, based on the assumption that labor dollars is the rational way to allocate overhead costs.

Our cost accounting now portrays the cost of producing widgets broken down into five elements:

1. Direct labor
   +
2. Direct materials
   +
3. Factory overhead
   +
4. Selling and marketing costs
   +
5. General and administrative costs
   =

   Total cost of producing widgets

Divide the total cost of producing widgets by the number of widgets produced and, *voilà*, you have the cost of producing one widget. How does that compare with the price we are charging for widgets? How does it compare with last year's cost?

Well, I really didn't mean to carry on so. I may have belabored the point, giving you more than you ever wanted to know about cost accounting, but it wasn't really that bad, was it? The important thing to keep in mind is this: Don't treat cost accounting as a neglected orphan in your accounting system. In the volatile, competitive economic world we inhabit, cost accounting is as necessary as a compass on a stormy sea. This holds true for small businesses as well as the big guys.

CHAPTER 30

HOW TO BUY A BUSINESS

WITHOUT GETTING HAD

Fools prepare the banquet.
The smart ones eat it.   Anonymous

Some people who want to be in business for themselves try for a running start by buying a business that already exists. This has advantages. First, it eliminates a competitor; stepping into someone else's shoes means there is one less person to split the local market pie.

Second, buying a business saves time. It takes years of thrashing around to develop facilities and contacts needed to establish a going business. Buying an existing one gives you a leg up.

Third, you may glean valuable tips and leads from the former owner. People who sell sometimes do so simply because they are worn out. For them, the rats are winning the rat race. They may have excellent experience and insight and well-formulated ideas for expanding and increasing profitability, but they may have run out of steam and can't keep it going anymore. You, being fresh to the fray, can take the ball and run with it.

Finally, buying an existing business is a golden opportunity to take advantage of long-term financing by negotiating a low down payment purchase contract with the former owner. Long-term debt is hard to come by in the world of small business. Buying a going concern under a stretched-out installment contract is one of the few chances you'll have to avail yourself of the leverage that long-term financing creates. There are two big problems, though, with buying a business.

1. First, it's a seller's market. Finding a decent business for sale isn't easy.

2. Second, establishing a fair price to pay is difficult, because valuing a small business involves subjective judgment.

Many businesses offered for sale are flea-bitten mutts on their way to the dog pound. Too often, the business is for sale because the current owner is trying to salvage something before he or she loses everything. But this isn't always the case. Sometimes good businesses are sold for legitimate reasons. The owner may want to retire or may have a health problem. Perhaps the owner has enough money and feels he or she can bail out and relax for a while. And, of course, even a "dog" may be worth considering if you can solve the previous owner's mistakes. Here are a few tips about finding a business to buy:

Accountants and lawyers are usually the first to know when a business owner wants to sell. Send a short letter to accountants and lawyers in the area where you want to be located. Describe the kind and size of business you are interested in and how much you expect to pay. If your first circularization doesn't bring a response, send another a few months later. Accountants and lawyers receive horrendous heaps of junk mail, so it takes persistence to get their attention.

Bankers are also good people to contact, but you should visit them in person. Bankers normally won't respond unless they see the whites of your eyes. Trade association directors know the latest gossip about association members, including whose company might be up for sale. If the type of business you are looking for has a trade association, contact its director. Classified ad sections of major newspapers contain listings of businesses for sale, although classifieds are definitely a long shot. Most worthwhile businesses change hands via word of mouth. They don't need to be advertised.

Some brokerage companies specialize in putting buyers and sellers together. They can be found in the Yellow Pages under the category of "Business Brokers." They act in the same capacity as real estate agents and work on a commission basis, usually taking 10 percent. Going through a business broker causes the purchase price to be higher because of the fee, but brokers do have the advantage of many contacts.

Finally, if you have the time and plenty of shoe leather, you can always go around knocking on doors. A good way to start is by consulting a business directory of the type used by marketing companies (sometimes called "SIC" lists because they categorize businesses by the standard industrial codes used by the federal government). One of the most prominent of these services is a company called Contacts Influential. SIC lists are "sucker lists" of businesses catalogued by size, type of business, and location. Besides giving addresses and telephone numbers, they characteristically include the date the company was founded, the number of employees, and the names of the principals. If you know someone who already subscribes to such a directory service, such as a stock broker, you may be able to talk the person into letting you use the directory for a small gratuity.

Earmark all of the businesses in the SIC list of the size and type you think you can handle. Then contact the owners and simply ask point blank if they'd like to sell. Wait until the end of the week before doing this, though. A business owner's inclination to sell the business is in direct proportion to the week's progression. After a rotten Monday, Tuesday, and Wednesday, you may catch the person in the right mood by Thursday or Friday.

Once you find a buy-out candidate, the next problem is determining what the business is worth. What is a reasonable price to pay? Take the Doozy Company, for example.

As you will recall, Doozy Company earned $20,000 after an owner's salary of $35,000 and had a book net worth of $145,000. However, taking into account the underlying value of its fixed assets, the company's real net worth was $230,000.

Now, how much is Doozy worth? How much would *you* pay for a $35,000 salary plus $20,000 of profits? The small business world's eternal question is, "How much should I pay for this company?" As a CPA, I constantly am asked this question, or the converse, "How much should I sell my company for?"

I have seen numerous businesses bought and sold. I have testified as an expert witness in court trials as to the value of businesses. I have attended seminars and read countless articles on the theory of small busi-

THE SECOND COMING OF THE WOOLLY MAMMOTH

ness valuation. I have fought the IRS over the estate tax values of businesses of deceased taxpayers. So, I should be a good person to ask, right? How much is this business worth? The answer is, I don't know! Furthermore, no one else knows, either. People who say they know are liars—or they are naive.

No one knows, because there *is* no answer. The original question was, "How much would *you* pay for this company?" The problem with this question is the word *you*. Ask 1,000 people the same question and you will get 1,500 different answers. (There's an extra 500 because half of the people will subsequently change their minds.)

The average of thousands of answers is how the marketplace determines the price of things. But there is no New York Stock Exchange for the purchase and sale of small businesses. There are only isolated buyers and isolated sellers. Furthermore, no two businesses are ever exactly alike. Small businesses can vary tremendously in their particulars, depending upon individual facts and circumstances. The price at which one changes hands depends upon the quirks, motives, idiosyncrasies, prejudices, and kookiness of the individuals involved. The value of a business, quite simply, is whatever someone is willing to pay for it. That is easy to define but hard to determine.

How do you ascertain the price that an informed, rational buyer will pay for a particular business? That relates pretty much to the future profits the buyer thinks the business will earn. In other words, what sort of return on their investment does the person expect?

As a practical matter, prices usually range somewhere between the liquidation value of the business (the minimum price) and ten times its average earnings (the maximum price).

Liquidation value is what would be left over after the smoke has cleared from a fire sale of the company's assets. That's the value often ascribed to a business that has been losing money or is in tough financial shape. If a business is profitable, it is usually valued by capitalizing its expected future earnings with a reasonable rate of return. Mathematically, the calculation is made by dividing anticipated average earnings of the business by the desired rate of return. This is known as the *capitalization of earnings* method. It is the most logical of any so-called formula approach.

The theory is this: If you put your money in a savings account at the bank, it will earn approximately five percent interest. Since five percent is the going rate for use of your money, the price you pay for a business should at least equal what it would take to make its earnings equal five percent of its purchase price. In Doozy's case that would be:

$$\text{Price} \times .05 = \$20,000 \text{ of earnings, or}$$
$$\text{Price} = \frac{\$20,000}{.05} = \$400,000$$

Pay $400,000 for the Doozy Company? Come on! No way! You think I'm crazy? Investing money in Doozy is not like putting it in a bank. Bank savings are safe and secure and can be withdrawn at any time. Investing in the likes of Doozy has substantial risks attached. It isn't hard at all to lose everything in a small business investment. Furthermore, Doozy's investment dollars are pretty much frozen. My money would likely stay put for a long period of time. Clearly, a higher rate of return should be used to reflect the fact that a Doozy-type investment is much riskier and less liquid than stashing money in a bank.

Capitalization formulas are often expressed in terms of the inverse. For example, the process of dividing earnings by five percent is the same thing as multiplying earnings by 20. You don't believe me? Try it.

$$\frac{1}{.05} = 20$$

$$\$20,000 \times 20 = \$400,000$$

In the Doozy example, we used a capitalization rate—or, as they say in the trade, a "cap rate"—of 20.

Capitalization rates for small business investments must be scaled down to take into account greater risk and less liquidity. Most small businesses change hands at prices less than 10 times earnings. Professional appraisers often wind up using a capitalization rate of four to five times the annual earnings of a small business, which equates to a 20 percent to 25 percent rate of return. That might seem like a high rate of return to expect, but you have to keep in mind the risks and headaches involved in running a small business enterprise.

A good guide as to an appropriate rate can be found in Dewing's Capitalization Rate Chart. Although this chart was published many years ago, Dewing's categories are still appropriate today. They are:

Cap Rate	Equivalent Rate of Return	Type of Business
10	10%	Old, very large businessses that are successful and have excellent goodwill. Very few come under this category.
8	12.5%	The same as the previous category, except considerable managerial care is required to run the company.
7	14.3%	Strong, well-established businesses sensitive to the general economy (vulnerable to recessions). They require strong managerial ability but little specialized knowledge on the part of executives.
5	20%	Medium-sized businesses requiring comparatively small capital investment and only average executive ability. They are highly competitive, but established goodwill is important.
4	25%	Small, highly competitive businesses requiring modest capital investment—the kind that practically anyone can start and manage.
2	50%	Large or small businesses that depend upon special or unusual skills of one manager or a small group of managers. They don't require much capital and are highly competitive with high mortality rates.
1	100%	Personal service businesses. They require modest amounts of capital, but the manager must have special skills and knowledge. The owner can sell the tangible part of the business, including its reputation, but cannot sell himself or herself, the only really valuable part of the enterprise.

As you can see, Dewing's Capitalization Rate Chart is not a precise formula. It is a guide toward making an educated guess. Following through on our example, here is how Doozy Company stacks up:

Doozy earned $20,000, but it is hardly fair to judge earning capacity on one year's performance. Doozy has ups and downs just like any small business. The average of several years is more indicative. The prior five years are usually considered a good base for averaging purposes. Doozy's past earnings look like this:

Last year	$ 20,000
Two years ago	20,000
Three years ago...	30,000
Four years ago	50,000
Five years ago	80,000
	$200,000

$200,000 divided by 5 years = $40,000 average annual earnings

Now we see that both the five-year average and last year's earnings are misleading. Doozy's $40,000 average is considerably more than last year's $20,000 profit, but earnings have been trending downward. To be fair, earnings should be given weight according to closeness in time to the present. Here is how that is done:

	Earnings	Weight Factor	Weighted Earnings
Last Year.........	$ 20,000 ×	5	= $100,000
Two years ago	20,000 ×	4	= 80,000
Three years ago...	30,000 ×	3	= 90,000
Four years ago	50,000 ×	2	= 100,000
Five years ago	80,000 ×	1	= 80,000
		15	$450,000

$450,000 divided by 15 =

$30,000 weighted average earnings

The weighted average of $30,000 is a better indicator of Doozy's earnings ability because it takes into account the trend.

Okay, what would you pay to receive $30,000 a year in earnings and a $35,000 salary? That depends upon how a $35,000 salary strikes you. If you are a $25,000-a-year person, $35,000 looks good. On the other hand, if your present salary is $45,000, $35,000 looks skimpy. In the latter case, you would likely consider Doozy's weighted average earnings to be only $20,000, because, in your eyes, the owner's salary should be increased by $10,000 to equal the $45,000 you feel you are worth.

This illustrates the fact that adjustments are often needed to make small business financial statements realistic. A small business owner's salary can vary tremendously. Owners' salaries depend upon income tax considerations, the working capital position of the company, personal standards of living, and the demands of one's spouse. You yourself must decide what is reasonable.

Other items can also cause distortions. A company may be using fast depreciation write-offs for tax purposes, and these may be greater than real economic depreciation. The company may have written off repair items to expense that should have been capitalized as permanent improvements. There may be unusual, one-shot items such as condemnation proceeds on real estate or damages collected from a lawsuit. Unrecognized bad debts may be hidden in accounts receivable. There may be severe distortions in income caused by inaccurate accounting for inventories. The point is, never accept a small business's financial statements as gospel. They must be analyzed and the figures must be verified.

But let's keep it simple. Let's assume $35,000 is a reasonable salary for Doozy and there are no quirks or bugs lurking in his accounting. Assume the figures are acceptable as stated. What capitalization rate do we use?

Doozy manufactures paperclips. That is a business not requiring much managerial talent or technical skill. It does require investment capital but not an enormous amount. Paperclip manufacturers are not affected by fluctuations in the economy, either local or national. Goodwill is not much of a factor since customers are not fussy about brand names. The product resembles a generic commodity. There is quite a bit of competition in the field, because many companies can manufacture paperclips and it is easy to increase production in response to demand.

Five years ago, Doozy made $80,000, but last year he netted only $20,000. After checking around, we discover Doozy went through a messy divorce. Then his girlfriend left him, so he has been hitting the bottle pretty heavy. Several business acquaintances believe he hasn't been tending to business. It appears that some conscientious management could reverse Doozy's declining earnings trend. For this reason, it isn't necessary to discount the purchase price for future profit shrinkage, because new management should be able to halt the downward trend. With these factors in mind, I would value Doozy Company using a cap rate of four times earnings—the fifth category on Dewing's chart. That would peg the price at $120,000 ($4 \times \$30,000 = \$120,000$).

"Hold on, there," you might declare. "A while back you said that Doozy Company's net worth was $230,000, taking into account the underlying value of its fixed assets. How can $230,000 of assets be bought for $120,000?"

They can't. Which is why net worth tends to be the minimum transfer price for a viable business. We would use net worth as the value here because it is higher than the capitalization of earnings formula. Doozy, you see, could merely liquidate his business and theoretically walk away with $230,000. Presumably, unless we can bamboozle him, we will have to pay at least that much to obtain his company.

This brings us to another consideration: the possibility that a company has assets not really connected with the business itself. It may own real estate or stocks held as passive investments. The company may have accumulated more working capital than it really needs. If so, these assets will have to be valued separate and apart from the business itself and added to the price arrived at for the pure operations.

The foregoing illustrates the sorts of things involved in determining the price to pay for a business. Other factors sometimes enter into it. For example, you'd probably be willing to pay more if seller's terms are generous, because a low down payment gives you leverage, thereby opening up the possibility of a higher rate of return on your investment. Occasionally, a bargain purchase may be possible if the owner is seriously ill or the business is in the hands of an estate.

Some businesses bring unexpectedly high prices because of monopolistic conditions. Professional sports franchises and radio stations are examples. They sell for ridiculously high prices based upon speculation that can't be justified by intrinsic value of earnings. Occasionally a business will be bought by another company at a premium price because the buying company anticipates being able to save costs by combining operations. These are called "strategic purchases."

Actually, it's fairly common for businesses to sell for more than capitalized earnings. In some industries, businesses change hands based upon code-of-the-hills formulas that involve gross sales or number of customers. Fuel oil companies sell for prices determined by total gallons of oil sold. Many service businesses customarily sell for one to two times annual gross revenue.

Code-of-the-hills prices have little direct relationship to company earnings. Yet, people pay them. Why is this, when such prices don't make sense economically? Most likely because some businesses are hard to start from scratch. Suppose you want to open an insurance agency. You have two choices: either hang up your shingle and starve to death for several years eating the wallpaper off the wall while waiting for clients to appear, or pay a bloated price for an existing agency—one or two times the annual renewal premiums. In effect, the inflated price reflects the start-up losses you would incur if you opened an agency with no customers. If you are stuck on the idea of owning an insurance business, those are your choices. If you don't care what kind of business you are in, you would reject buying an insurance company, because you'd get a better return purchasing a business whose price is based upon its earnings potential.

How do you know if a code-of-the-hills formula exists for the type of business you contemplate? Owners of such businesses will clue you in real fast if you make a purchase inquiry. For additional background as to what is customary, check with the director of the industry's trade association located nearest your geographic area. Most libraries carry the *Encyclopedia of Associations*, which lists names and addresses of trade associations.

When a business's purchase price does exceed what its earnings justify, your only hope for a decent return is either to build it up, in which case you will have paid the seller for something you yourself create, or to try to sell it later for an even higher inflated value. This means you will be speculating on an arbitrary increase in value rather than buying earnings potential. This is fine, as long as you realize up-front that this is the game being played and that the speculation bubble doesn't burst. Here are some random thoughts and comments about buying a business:

1. As to the kind of business to buy, stick to one you know something about. It's hard enough being on your own as it is, but if you are a greenhorn with the business you buy, you are rolling dice with Old Man Disaster.

2. If you stubbornly insist on getting involved with something unfamiliar, then take the time to become acquainted. Work as an apprentice for a while. There are tricks of the trade for every business. Large companies can afford to hire technical brains, but small business owners have to be personally familiar with all aspects of their business.

3. Important! Important! Important! Be sure you are buying profits instead of a job. Suppose you come to me looking for work and I say, "Sure, I have a job for you. I'll pay you $30,000 a year. But I want you to pay me $120,000 for the opportunity to have the job." You would suggest I take a flying leap at the moon, right? Why is it any different buying a business? Suppose a seller tells you that he or she makes $30,000 a year and wants $120,000 for the business. That's what the business is worth, using a four-times-earnings cap rate, isn't it? Absolutely not, because the seller hasn't deducted an allowance for his or her own salary. Say the seller's services are worth $25,000. That means the business really is making only $5,000, which makes it worth $20,000 on a formula basis. Yet, I see people all of the time who would be willing to pay the inflated $120,000 asking price because they overlook this principle.

4. Always have the former owner sign a noncompetition agreement as part of the deal. That way, the seller can't change his or her mind next month and open up down the street as a competitor.

5. Stay clear of businesses that have only a few major customers. Nothing is so vulnerable as a small business dependent upon a narrow customer base. Its sales volume can evaporate overnight.

6. If you are dickering with a corporation, it is usually best to buy the corporation's assets and goodwill rather than its capital stock. In other words, buy specific assets rather than the corporate entity itself. That way, you know what you've got. If you buy the corporation, you inherit skeletons in the closet, ghosts in the attic, and creepy-crawlies in the basement—such as latent tax deficiencies, lawsuits, or other claims that haven't yet jelled at the time of closing.

7. Be sure an environmental survey is performed on any property owned by the business being bought. As its new owner, you will be liable for hazardous waste problems that exist at the time of purchase, even if the problems were created by someone else!

8. Hire your own lawyer and accountant to represent you and to help analyze the deal. Never depend upon the seller's professional advisors. How can they serve you and their client at the same time? And don't depend upon your own wits either. You'd better believe the bit about "He who represents himself has a fool for a client." There are many points in the fine print of a sales agreement that only an attorney will know how to handle. Some examples are seller's warranties and indemnifications, default provisions, contract terms, escrow arrangements, and noncompetition agreements. Plus, your attorney should search for the existence of liens and lawsuits. And analyzing and verifying the seller's financial statements should be left to the talents of a sharp, aggressive accountant.

9. Obtain written warranties from the seller for the veracity of his or her representations regarding all aspects of the business, particularly the accuracy of financial statements and other financial records.

10. Hold back part of the purchase price until you've had a chance to operate the business for a while. This puts you in a stronger bargaining position should some of the seller's representations turn out to be blue mud and canal water.

11. It has been my experience that most people pay too much when purchasing a business. Finding a decent one to buy isn't easy. Consequently, when a person finds a prospect, he or she tends to overvalue it because of its scarcity. That's a mistake. We are not dealing with precious gems or antiques. Unless it is a monopolistic situation, a business doesn't gain value simply because there aren't many for sale. Always remember, the intrinsic value of a business depends upon the rate of return it gives the owner—and nothing more.

    I can say this all I want, and it is perfectly logical to say it; but the fact is, buyers are inclined to pay a premium for a business regardless of the shape it is in just because it exists. When a person has been searching for a long time, he or she tends to become overly anxious and pays a premium out of frustration. People tend to fall in love once they find a viable buy-out candidate. They want so badly to own their own businesses that they become emotionally involved, sometimes almost to the point of being like an animal in heat.

12. Above all else, take your time. Beat the bushes and shake the trees, but don't be in a hurry to pick up the first deal that falls to the ground. Purchase of a business will be one of the biggest financial commitments of your life. Take the time to investigate everything thoroughly. Don't be pressured into a quick decision for fear of missing an opportunity. Small businesses are like buses. If you miss one now, another will come along later.

Two partners were eking out a precarious existence in a small furniture manufacturing company. They were overjoyed one day to receive an unexpected million-dollar order from a large department store chain. The new business would insure their survival, but there was a hitch: The order was subject to cancellation within 60 days if the department store changed its mind.

The two partners waited with bated breath for 60 days to pass. The closer it got to the deadline, the more they bit their fingernails. Fifty-eight days passed, then 59 days passed. On the 60th day, an important looking telegram arrived.

The first partner covered his eyes with his hands and said, "I can't stand it, Sam. Open it and tell me what it says." Sam's shaky fingers tore open the envelope. "Good news!" shouted Sam. "It says your brother died!"

CHAPTER 31

HOW MUCH WORKING CAPITAL

DO YOU REALLY NEED?

Happiness is having ten cents . . . in front of a pay toilet.   Rochelle Davis

Every so often, a bright-eyed, bushy-tailed neophyte—who thinks he or she has it all figured out—wanders into my office. Typically, the neophyte has lined up enough money to buy a little equipment, some supplies, and a few weeks' payroll. He or she has carefully calculated that the first month's sales will generate enough money to pay for the second month's operating expenses. The second month's sales will pay for the third month's expenses, the third month's sales will pay for the fourth month's expenses, and so on. The neophyte figures he or she can keep going like that, living hand-to-mouth, month-to-month while profits gradually accumulate.

Dreamer! Get serious. There is a time lag between the point expenses are incurred and the point they are converted into salable products. There is another time lag between the creation of the salable product and the time the product is sold. And there is a time lag between sales and the point you collect the money.

In other words, a significant time interval elapses before money leaving your pocket comes back in the form of cash. This is known as a company's business cycle. Business cycles usually last five or six months, although they vary quite a bit from business to business. Business cycles mean you need more working capital than you might expect, which is why investing in a business involves much more than buying hard assets. You also have to invest in accounts receivable, inventory, and prepaid expenses. And you must have enough cash to pay current operating expenses. As far as your business is concerned, these are permanent fixed assets too, just as much as buildings and equipment.

To illustrate, here is how that rookie neophyte who walked into my office figured the business's cash budget for the first two months of operations:

Neophyte's Cash Budget
First Two Months' Operations

	First Month	Second Month
Beginning Cash ....$	–0–	$2,000
Cash Receipts		
Capital invested by owner....	5,000	–
Bank loan	5,000	–
Equipment loan.............	10,000	–
Sales proceeds	2,000	8,000
	22,000	8,000
Cash Disbursements		
Cost of equipment...........	(15,000)	–
Cost of labor and materials...	(3,500)	(3,500)
Cost of overhead	(1,000)	(1,000)
Cost of supplies	(500)	–
Equipment loan payment	–	(500)
	(20,000)	(5,000)
Ending Cash ....$	2,000	$5,000

THE SECOND COMING OF THE WOOLLY MAMMOTH

Looking good. According to this, $5,000 will be on hand after two months. Enough to pay off the bank loan. Nice try, but here is how it really works out:

Grizzled Old Pro's Cash Budget
First Two Months' Operations

	First Month	Second Month
Beginning Cash ....$	–0–	$ (1,000)
Cash Receipts		
Capital invested by owner....	5,000	–
Bank loan	5,000	–
Equipment loan.............	10,000	–
Sales proceeds	1,000	5,000
	21,000	5,000
Cash Disbursements		
Cost of equipment..........	(15,000)	(500)
Cost of labor and materials...	(4,000)	(5,000)
Cost of overhead	(250)	(1,750)
Cost of supplies	(750)	(250)
Utility deposits	(500)	–
Rent deposit	(500)	–
Legal and registration fees ...	(500)	–
Installation costs for equip. ..	(500)	–
Equipment loan payment	–	(500)
	(22,000)	(8,000)
Ending Cash (overdraft) ....$	(1,000)	$ (4,000)

The neophyte's $5,000 cash surplus evaporates into a $4,000 bank overdraft, just like that! Zippo, presto! But wait! There is more to come. Would you believe there is a $3,000 *profit* despite the $4,000 cash shortage? Watch.

Two Months' Income Statement

Sales....................	$ 16,000
Materials and Supplies...	(6,000)
Labor...................	(4,000)
Overhead	(3,000)
Net Income	3,000

To prove that a $3,000 profit does, indeed, coexist with a $4,000 cash deficit, here is the balance sheet:

Balance Sheet at the End of Two Months

Assets

Cash...........................	$ −0−
Accounts receivable	10,000
Inventory......................	2,500
Deposits and prepaid expenses...	1,000
Equipment	15,500
Organization expense	500
Total Assets	$ 29,500

Liabilities

Bank overdraft	$ 4,000
Accounts payable and accured expenses	$ 3,000
Bank note	5,000
Equipment contract	9,500
Total Liabilities...............	21,500

Net Worth

Capital invested by owner........	5,000
Net profit......................	3,000
	8,000
Total Liabilities and Net Worth.....	$29,500

THE SECOND COMING OF THE WOOLLY MAMMOTH

The owner runs out of cash even though the business starts out profitable. The problem, of course, is that the owner raised only $20,000 of capital ($5,000 from the owner's own resources and $15,000 borrowed from the bank), which is $10,000 short of what was actually needed. Still, $20,000 is quite a bit of money. I wonder what happened to it. What happened? Aha! Come out of the phone booth, Mr. Cash Flow Statement; here is a job for you.

Cash Flow Statement
First Two Months' Operations

Beginning Cash		$	–0–
Cash Flow from Operations			
Net income, accrual basis ....$	3,000		
Adjustments for non-cash transactions			
Increase in accounts receivable........	(10,000)		
Increase in inventory.................	(2,500)		
Increase in accounts payable	3,000		
Cash basis income (deficit)...........		(6,500)	
Cash Flow from Investments			
Purchase of equipment	(15,500)		
Deposits and organization expense	(1,500)	(17,000)	
Cash Flow from Financing			
Owner's investment	5,000		
Bank loan	5,000		
Equipment loan......................	10,000		
Equipment loan payments	(500)	19,500	
Ending Cash (overdraft)		($ 4,000)	

Woe, and a dark cloud cometh over the land. No money and a big pile of bills! The moral is: People starting out in business invariably underestimate the time lag involved in their business cycle. They forget about having to invest in accounts receivable and inventories. They compound this by overestimating beginning sales and underestimating expenses. "Everything cost more than we thought it would!" is the universal lament of *nouveau* business people.

It's easy to be overly optimistic when starting out. As a matter of fact, optimism is necessary or you probably wouldn't even try going out on your own. Unfortunately, this nearly always causes entrepreneurs to wind up needing more working capital than they counted on. As a rule of thumb, you'd better add a 50 percent fudge factor to whatever capital you initially decide is necessary.

Don't count on profits to solve your working capital problem either. Paradoxically, early profits can actually increase cash shortages, as the foregoing example just showed. When sales are greater than expected, it means more inventory, accounts receivable, overhead, and equipment. As a result, a business that expands too rapidly can have a cash problem just as critical as that of a business losing money.

Of course, being profitable and short of cash is far preferable to needing cash because you are losing money. It is light-years easier to borrow the short-fall from a bank if you are profitable. Furthermore, if profits continue long enough, they eventually will catch up to your business cycle. But waiting for this to happen can cause anxious moments.

Budgeting and estimating cash flows are not exact sciences. I don't care how smart you are or how realistic you try to be; the future always holds surprises. But anticipating problems ahead of time will cause you to be sharper. In business, running scared spitless is preferable to starting out overconfident.

PART FIVE

EFFICIENT OPERATIONS, AS TAUGHT BY

HARD-KNOCKS UNIVERSITY

CHAPTER 32

THE MIRACLES OF CLEVER MARKETING

Advertising may be described as the science of
stopping human intelligence long enough to
get money from it.   Stephen Leacock

There are three questions small business people should ask themselves continually:

1. *Who* is my potential customer?

2. *What* do I have that he or she wants?

3. *How* can I get my foot in the door?

That is the guts of marketing. Ironically, hardly anyone ever thinks in these terms other than marketing specialists. Consider the following example:

A prepackaged food manufacturing company developed a line of pre-cooked, frozen gourmet meals. The company tried to sell these products through shops specializing in gourmet food. And why not? The product was gourmet food, wasn't it? But sales were miserable and the company's new line bombed. Meanwhile, a competitor introduced a similar product but distributed it through supermarkets. The competitor's product went over like gangbusters.

How come? Company Number One thought its customers were gourmet cooks. Wrong, wrong, wrong. Its real customers were busy people interested in convenience: harried housewives, career women, and single men—the habitual buyers of easy-to-prepare supermarket food.

THE SECOND COMING OF THE WOOLLY MAMMOTH

In contrast, those interested in specialty foods enjoy subtleties of "from scratch" cooking. Convenience food, whether gourmet or not, doesn't float their boat. Time savings is not a big factor in their food buying decisions. The first company blew it by failing to recognize this distinction. It didn't comprehend the reality of who its potential customers were.

Obviously, it was selling gourmet food, but only secondarily. The primary thing it was selling was convenience. Where do people look to buy that? They look in the very outlets the company ignored when marketing its product: in supermarkets and convenience stores.

This illustrates small business naivete toward marketing. Big businesses are more sophisticated. As a matter of fact, they take it several steps further. Big companies often use marketing principles to mislead people. The famous Bartles & Jaymes wine cooler TV ads are a classic example. The ads feature those marvelously hokey country bumpkins, taciturn "Ed Jaymes" and his down-home "Thank'u fer yer support" companion, "Frank Bartles." It's a tremendously clever and fabulously successful ad campaign.

The ads hawk a wine cooler, right? Nope. Guess again. They sell image—nostalgic visions of small-town, small-company values and virtues, the wistful idea that Bartles & Jaymes is made by honest, straightforward, countrified folk. Buying a bottle of their wine cooler is portrayed as being like dealing with a neighborhood lemonade stand. Because that's what the company thinks will sell. Its advertising campaign seduces your focus away from the fact that Bartles & Jaymes is manufactured by the world's biggest wine company, Ernest and Julio Gallo winery! The rationale behind the advertising campaign is why you need an electron microscope to find Gallo's name on a Bartles & Jaymes bottle.

The interesting thing is this: Even though we're all hip and chuckle at such witty, tongue-in-cheek stuff, the image sticks! Exposure to the ads causes us to feel good looking at Bartles & Jaymes bottles. This illustrates the importance of image. Even heavy-handed facetiousness has an impact.

Business school curricula pay short shrift to marketing concepts. That's a pity as well as being unjust. Be ye butcher, baker, or candlestick maker, business success depends upon your Music Man abilities. We are all, in the last analysis, salespeople.

Not being a marketing expert myself, you will have to look elsewhere for a comprehensive marketing education. But I do want to emphasize its importance and acquaint you with its fundamental principles. Among small business people, marketing concepts often go unrecognized. Consequently, if you devote some attention to the subject, you will have a nice edge over competitors.

Small business marketing usually consists of garish signs on storefronts and tasteless ads in local newspapers. That, plus passing out cheap pens with the firm's logo and sponsoring little league teams. What most entrepreneurs don't realize is that marketing involves much more than advertising gimmicks and trinkets. There are several different elements involved, which should be incorporated into an integrated approach.

1. Determine exactly what it is you are going to peddle in the way of a product or service (intangible as well as tangible).

2. Determine who are the logical customers for your product and how you're going to lay your stuff on them. (In other words, determine your distribution system.)

3. Establish the prices you think you can get away with.

4. Try to forecast future sales and demand.

5. Figure out how to pay salespeople and sales reps in a way that lights their fire. (In other words, provide incentive compensation.)

6. Come up with some whiz-bang promotional and prospecting activities (advertising, sales promotion, and public relations).

Here are a few comments based upon my observations and personal experiences:

As to the product being sold, most small business people see no further than a few inches in front of their nose. They focus on the two-dimensional skin of their product rather than four-dimension reality. If asked what they do for a living, they say, "I sell Ganipganops." The fact is, that is only part of what they sell. Almost every service or product has more than one component. In addition to physical qualities, products have an aura that people can't see but can sense and feel. Business people often overlook the psychological aspects surrounding their product, because these qualities are intangible. Yet, these qualities are real. You can bet their customers recognize them, subconsciously if not consciously.

IBM sells much more than computers. It also sells support and service and reliability and continuity, which is why it gets premium prices. People are willing to pay for those things. IBM's marketing makes sure potential customers realize they are receiving a generous helping of intangibles as well as hardware in a big box.

I continuously have to remind younger members of our CPA firm that we don't sell tax returns and financial statements. Small business clients don't get turned on perusing numbers. The figures themselves are relatively esoteric. The true intrinsic value of what we sell lies in personalized answers delivered with a bedside manner. The key is to provide services by someone who cares. That is what small business people are interested in. Do you see what I am getting at? You must look beyond the physical package to see what it is you are really selling.

As to the product itself, a small business person's objective is to find a niche, an underexploited opportunity, a target market. Markets can be defined according to a number of different criteria, such as:

1. Geographic location (national, regional, state, local)

2. The benefits people seek (security, safety, amusement)

3. Demographics (age, sex, income)

4. Psychographics (life-styles, personality traits, and so on)

5. Behaviorisms (user status, loyalty)

6. Customer size (major accounts, dealer accounts, individual consumers)

7. Price

8. Quality

The first step is to analyze those market segments applicable to the area of your business interest. The emphasis should be on markets rather than products. The most profitable form of niche searching is to look for a market in need of a product rather than a product in need of a market.

THE SECOND COMING OF THE WOOLLY MAMMOTH

A better mousetrap would be a hot item because people have problems with mice, but the world won't beat a path to your door for inventing a trap that catches hedgehogs, regardless how clever it might be.

Let's jump ahead and assume you've found a niche, identified your potential customer, developed a product, determined its tangible and intangible aspects, and are ready to roll. "Look out, world, here I come." But aren't you forgetting something? What are you going to charge? What price tag do you put on the product?

Pricing is often academic because small businesses frequently find themselves governed by what the market will bear. What has to be determined, though, is whether the going market price allows you a decent living. If it doesn't, seek another opportunity, because you can't lose five cents a gallon and make it up on volume.

For example, many women who want to start their own business contemplate opening a small dress shop or boutique. Unfortunately, small retail shops of this nature usually turn out to be losers. This is because prices are established by major retailers. Big stores determine what prices the market will bear based upon volume buying and volume selling. A small dress shop has a difficult time charging enough to make a decent profit, because it can't achieve the necessary volume to make it on low-margin merchandise.

The only way a small shop can be profitable is to sell something that big stores don't—whether it's specialized merchandise or an intangible such as a convenient location, favorable store hours, or better service. The question then becomes: Can those things be sold for enough to offset low-margin merchandise?

On the other hand, it happens occasionally that a small business creates a new product or service that is novel enough to have little initial competition. Then the opposite problem arises: the business charges less than what the market will bear!

The initial period of a new product or service is what marketing experts call the "skim" phase. Some might propose "rip-off" is a more appropriate term, but that's being cynical. From the standpoint of practical economics, prices during the skim phase should be based upon intrinsic value to the customer rather than costs to produce. Many small business people think in terms of "moral" prices. Something in the neighborhood of two times manufacturing costs is customarily thought to be reasonable and, therefore, is the appropriate price even though more could be charged. This is misguided philosophy. Not taking advantage of the skim phase gives competitors a better chance to catch up.

Theoretically, accurate sales forecasts are a great help for planning business operations—if you can figure out a way of doing them, that is. Big business forecasting methods range from naive extrapolations of current sales to consumer surveys to historical analogies to computer-generated econometric models. Whatever the approach, forecasting usually requires technical sophistication and data availability beyond the resources of most small businesses.

Some small businesses can forecast sales because of unique attributes peculiar to their line of business. Fuel oil companies, for example, can accurately predict future consumption based upon the moving average of daily temperatures. All they need is a thermometer, a simple calculator, and some prior history. Unfortunately, forecasting is "iffy" for most other small businesses. I mention it here only because it is an academic consideration among marketing people.

As to compensating salespeople, the important thing is incentive. Incentive to perform. Incentive to beat one's brains out for the company, to sacrifice oneself for the cause, to ask "How high?" when asked to jump. But to be effective, an incentive must have immediate and direct impact. So don't defer incentive compensation too far in the future. If you are going to put carrots in front of salespeople, you will get more miles per carrot if you dangle it right in front of the sales person's nose rather than placing it in a box that won't be opened until Christmas.

Last, we come to the subject people usually think of first when marketing is mentioned: promotional advertising. The root cause of urban-blight tackiness. Every town has it. Cluttered strips of roadway lined with winking, blinking plastic signs and reader boards, interspersed with tethered balloons, neon lettering, and flapping plastic streamers. Outrageous examples of do-it-yourself advertising. As folk art it is interesting, but as advertising it is ineffectual.

Everyone nowadays is aware that most people remember something if it is repeated to them 20 times or more, and that most of what we learn comes through our sense of sight. This is such common knowledge it has become the magnificent obsession of small business people. Like rain-coated flashers, most shopkeepers have a mania for displaying themselves before the passing public. Hence, the plethora of trashy signs yelling for our attention. But the key to advertising is effectiveness rather than prominence. This means portraying a message as well as making potential customers aware of your existence. It also means sending your message to the intended target rather than the world at large.

If potential customers constitute only one percent of the public, why spend big bucks for Yellow Page advertising that hits 100 percent of the public? Why not use advertising dollars on something that circulates specifically among your intended markets, such as special subject magazines or neighborhood newspapers? Or, how about direct mailouts to selected potential customers?

Does it ever occur to Joe Average small business person that surveying existing customers might be very illuminating? Like having his customers tell him where they came from and how they found out about him and why they patronize him. It's a simple thing to do, but small business people hardly ever do it. Yet, wouldn't that information show where the business's advertising firepower should be aimed? Think about it.

The most effective advertising, though, is an existing customer who is sublimely satisfied. Never forget that. The tendency is to focus efforts on enticing new customers in the front door rather than keeping old ones from walking out the back. Your best bet is to concentrate time and money on making existing customers happy. They are your most likely source of new business. Besides, it costs five times as much to get a new customer as it does to keep an existing one, according to marketing experts.

Finally, as you proceed through life eagerly huckstering your product, always remember the cardinal principle of successful promoters: People soon forget most of what they hear you say, but they will always remember how you made them feel when you were saying it.

THE SECOND COMING OF THE WOOLLY MAMMOTH

It is often said that no one ever went broke underestimating the average man's taste or overestimating his greed. Maximizing these factors without crossing the border into Sleazeville is one of the biggest problems in marketing.

CHAPTER 33

PROFESSIONAL ADVISORS

Why does New Jersey have more criminals but fewer attorneys than New York? Because New Jersey got first choice.   Old lawyer joke

What's the definition of an accountant? Someone who would have been an actuary but couldn't pass the personality test.   Old accountant joke

Maxim: Never trust a lawyer or a CPA under 35 years of age.

Corollary: Never trust a lawyer or a CPA over 50 years of age.

Believe it or not, law and accounting are intellectually demanding. There is much to know and learn these days. Academic training isn't enough. Until someone has 10 years of practical experience, he or she just isn't worth much. So, don't hire professional advisors unless they are at least 35. By that age, professionals will have stubbed their toes many times—at someone else's expense. By coming along later, you will benefit from hard-earned experience that others have paid for.

The intense demands of the legal and accounting professions cause early flame-outs. By age 50, any lawyer or CPA specializing in small business will have been through a lot and won't feel like going through much more. Twenty-five years of long hours, tensions, frustrations, unreasonable clients, and modest pay will have taken their toll. By age 50, a lawyer or a CPA usually has junior associates doing the dirty work. Unless you are an important client, you'll never have the benefit of the older guy's experience. The older advisor will have brief conferences with you now and then, but some green-as-grass grunt in the back office will be doing your work. You are better off hiring middle-aged professional advisors between the ages of 35 and 50—still young enough to have some piss and vinegar but old enough to dilute it with wisdom.

About professional fees: You may not always get what you pay for, but for darn sure you will always pay for what you get. A lawyer or a CPA who is any good won't work cheap. So don't shop for the lowest bidder. Cheap fees mean cheap work. Deep-discount legal and accounting services backfire in the long run. Faulty advice or non-advice will cost you more than any fees you save. As John Ruskin wrote:

> It's unwise to pay too much, but it's worse to pay too little. When you pay too much, you lose a little money, that is all. When you pay too little, you sometimes lose everything, because the thing you bought is incapable of doing the thing it was bought to do. The common law of business balance prohibits paying a little and getting a lot—it can't be done. If you deal with the lowest bidder, it is well to add something for the risk you run. And if you do that, you will have enough to pay for something better.

Find out the professionals' fee arrangement in advance. That way there shouldn't be any surprises. They probably can't give an accurate estimate because it is hard to predict ahead of time how many hours will be involved, but at least they should be able to give you a rough idea.

Most people use the wrong criteria when seeking a professional advisor. Be it accountant, lawyer, doctor, or auto mechanic, if there are several candidates to choose from, people invariably go for the one they relate to personally. It's human nature. I've done this a number of times myself. That's how we elect presidents, isn't it? By the cut of their jib and the jive of their talk rather than the content of what they say. But there is no correlation between personality and professional competence.

Acquiring insight into a professional's proficiency is possible if you take the time to make enough inquiries. Ask local bankers and other business people whom they would recommend. If you can discover the identities of existing and former clients, seek out some of them and ask their impressions. One opinion isn't worth much, but if you sample enough people, patterns may emerge. This is a more rational way to choose a professional than "gut" feel.

Generally speaking, it's harder to find a good CPA than a good lawyer.

That is because CPAs are harder to judge. The typical CPA personality resembles tap water—colorless, tasteless, and odorless. Public accounting is the Rodney Dangerfield of professions. If you are looking for an antonym to *charisma*, use *CPA*. There has never been a CPA equivalent to the TV series "L.A. Law" or "St. Elsewhere," and the only movie that featured CPAs was *Revenge of the Nerds*.

After you've hired a lawyer and a CPA, you'll generally find out relatively soon if they are any good. Doctors bury their mistakes, but you stand a better chance with lawyers and CPAs. They try to conceal their goofs, but because of the overt nature of their work product, it is easier to catch them at it. If you're curious about how they handled something or the way it turned out, ask them for an explanation. Chances are, you won't understand the finer points of their answers. But if they use weasel words or "bomfog" generalities, watch out!

The key to getting your money's worth from professional advisors is to use them as preventative medicine. See your lawyer and CPA *before* you do something, not after—especially your lawyer. I see business people all of the time wallowing in legal cesspools they could have avoided if they hadn't been too cheap to consult an attorney.

A lawyer's real value is in helping you *avoid* fights rather than in being a hired gun. Lawsuits can be frightfully expensive. They are also very trying on the nerves. I can't emphasize too much the importance of trying to dodge them. Despite the virtuousness of your case, you always stand a chance of losing once you are in the courtroom. Business disputes frequently result in capricious judgments, because they often involve issues that judges, juries, and attorneys don't fully understand.

Newcomers to business tend to regard business disputes as affairs of honor. Not going to court over an issue means losing face. Forget it. What good is saving face if you lose your pants in the process? Vindicating one's position in the business world is a time-consuming, costly luxury. Sometimes you can't escape winding up in court, but try to conduct your affairs so as to make it a rare occurrence. The key is to consult your attorney ahead of time and often. A few minutes of conversation can save hours of grief and frustration. The same thing applies to using an accountant. People continually come into my office with tax problems they wouldn't have had if they had seen me *before* they did the deal. But how do you re-ring the bell once it's been gonged?

America's Byzantine legal system is driving people to seek practical alternatives to litigation, sometimes referred to as the Alternative Dispute Resolution (ADR) movement. The process of settling arguments through mediation and arbitration is rapidly gaining in popularity. Mediation involves negotiating through a neutral third party, who, by introducing a bit of adult supervision into the dispute, helps the parties find a mutually agreeable solution. Mediation is private, informal, and voluntary.

Arbitration is a more formal process, because the parties usually agree in advance to be bound by the arbitrator's decision. The disputants choose an impartial arbitrator (or arbitrators) knowledgeable in the matters at hand to hear each side and issue a binding opinion. Arbitrators are often chosen through the auspices of the American Arbitration Association, which has branches in most major cities. Because arbitration proceedings are less structured than a courtroom, much time and money is saved. More importantly, intelligent decisions are more likely because the arbitrator has specific expertise in the disputed area. In contrast, it often happens that judges and juries are unacquainted with specific business issues.

As long as we are discussing professional advisors, something should be said about business consultants. What will be said is this: consultants at the small business level are usually a waste of money. A number of my clients have hired so-called consultants and their experiences have been disappointing.

The idea of hiring an "expert" has great appeal when a pack of yapping problems are nipping at your behind. Unfortunately, many consultants catering to small business are really just professional magic-wand wavers. They say, "I am the Great Exalted Wizard, an infallible brain. Hire me and I will prevail over your most pressing problems." Then they switch on their smoke-and-mirrors machine. As a practical matter, consultants in this category usually give their clients nothing more than "jargon-ated," cliché-ridden enumeration of problems the client is already aware of.

Years ago, before management consulting became the high-priest type activity it presently is, a prominent management consultant explained his practice as being mainly the application of common sense. That honest insight still holds true today, especially where small business consulting is concerned. So don't count on a business consultant having any special magic or divine insights to offer. If the consultant is a real whiz-bang, he or she probably won't accept small business engagements to begin with because the fees are too small.

Let's get back to lawyers and accountants. Here are some things you'd better have your attorney do for you:

1. Help you decide on the form of doing business.

2. Draft a written partnership agreement.

3. Draft a buy-sell agreement with your partners or fellow stockholders.

4. Review contracts and agreements *before* you sign them.

5. Review the details of long-term financing arrangements.

6. Review the legal ramifications of any new ventures you are thinking of undertaking.

Here are some things you should have your CPA do for you:

1. Set up your accounting system.

2. Set up a system of internal control for your assets.

3. Help you with loan application presentations.

4. Represent you before the Internal Revenue Service. (Don't talk to the IRS yourself. IRS agents are highly skilled at getting people simultaneously to shoot themselves in one foot while shoving the other in their mouth.)

5. Periodically review your books and analyze your financial statements.

6. Help you prepare budgets and projections.

Finally, make sure your attorney and CPA earn their fees, but don't begrudge it to them. Very few who service small business clientele die wealthy, believe me.

CHAPTER 34

THE CARE AND FEEDING OF EMPLOYEES

*The experienced business manager knows his employees
will include neurotics, self-seekers, incompetents and
prima donnas. His success as a business manager is
measured by his ability to take this unpromising amalgam
and get the job done with the least amount of
mayhem.* Anonymous

Be aware of employees' egos. The biggest cause of dissatisfaction isn't low pay or poor working conditions. It's feeling insignificant, thinking what they are doing is piddling and unimportant. Insensitive bosses foster this perception by creating the impression that their employees aren't needed as individuals, that they are small cogs. Don't take employees or their work for granted. Puff up their egos when their work warrants it. Blast them when they fall down on the job, but don't just ignore them. Remember, a few judicious compliments stimulate incentive as much as a raise.

Much has been made of Japanese management methods. American companies have stood in awe as their Japanese counterparts ran productivity circles around them. At first, U.S. industry thought mysterious Far East secrets were being applied. Zen Buddhism, perhaps? Much to America's chagrin, it turns out there are no secrets! It's merely a case of conscientiously and vigorously applying old-fashioned, commonsense notions about human nature.

Japanese excel at making company employees feel they are a vital part of the organization, from the lowest levels to the highest. Japanese companies emphasize participation in management decisions and provide employees with feedback. They solicit suggestions and are concerned for their health and welfare. They create an atmosphere of teamwork rather than the usual class warfare of labor versus middle management, and middle management versus executives. In other words, they emphasize treating people like people. Why is everyone so amazed this works?

What about dog-eat-dog and devil-take-the-hindmost being the best motivators? There is no question productivity is enhanced when people are beaten with sticks to produce. And having to compete with people trying to steal your job is most certainly an incentive of the highest order. But research indicates internal incentives are greater motivators than those of the external variety. Particularly situations that involve cooperative efforts—for example, when people you care about are depending upon you and you are depending upon them.

Anyone involved in team sports will vouch that this is so. Something special happens when rapport exists throughout a team and everyone is united in a cooperative effort. It's a special kind of magic when this happens. Concern for not letting one's buddies down transcends individual interests. The point is, trying to do one's best to beat out others is not necessarily the same as trying to do one's best.

Isn't that what the Japanese management system is all about—involving employees as team members in the company enterprise? U.S. auto manufacturers seem to think so. Most of them are now scurrying around trying Japanese methods on for size. In fact, auto workers' unions are now worried that adoption of Japanese team concepts by manufacturers will eliminate animosity between labor and management, thereby reducing union influence.

Weyerhaueser, the forest products giant, recently opened a new veneer plant. If you plucked an old-time mill hand out of retirement and sat him down in the new plant, he would rub his eyes in disbelief. Get this. There are no supervisors. That is because there are no jobs for them. The traditional supervisor's position in managerial hierarchy is occupied by so-called team leaders. Team leaders don't tell workers what to do and don't hover around making sure workers' noses stay in contact with the grindstone. Their avowed purpose in life is to provide information, set objectives, measure results, and assist worker "teams" in solving problems.

There are no foremen, either. The foreman's role is assigned to so-called core team members who are elected by worker team members. The plant is non-union and everyone receives a salary instead of an hourly wage. Pay is based on an incentive system that goes up and down, depending upon productivity and profitability. Workers are trained to do several jobs rather than just one specialty—whether it is operating a machine, doing equipment repairs, programming a computer, or welding a seam.

The system emphasizes open communications, and lines of demarcation between jobs and workers and management are as undelineated as possible. Regular meetings and bulletin board postings keep workers apprised of all aspects of plant operations. Input from workers is encouraged. Participatory management, they call it. The new mill is modeled after Japanese auto manufacturing plants. Although it is radical, relative to traditional American factory concepts, Weyerhaueser feels it is the wave of the future in terms of making the U.S. competitive.

Creating a Japanese-style "team" attitude among employees sounds great, but what happens if you have a rotten team? Columbia University's football team presumably has as much solidarity and unanimity as its competition. Yet, every Saturday the hapless Lions set another NCAA record for losses. Obviously, team spirit is no substitute for competence and in and of itself won't get you out of the bottom ten. So, before clasping employees to your company's breast, hire a qualified crew. For example, Weyerhaueser screens the workers it hires for its new veneer plant as carefully as it screens upper-level managers.

But the secret to good hiring is good firing. Competent, conscientious employees are hard to find. Most of the time, you'll have to try several people before finding the right one. That means going through a cycle of hiring and firing. Many small business people choke up when it comes to the firing part. It's unpleasant having to ash-can someone, so many bosses avoid it except when gross provocation is involved. Consequently, they wind up accumulating marginal employees and having to rationalize their weaknesses: "Well, Sam makes quite a few mistakes all right, and he's not too good handling customers sometimes, but he's been with us 10 years now and knows the business real well. It would probably take a long time to train somebody to replace him and, besides, he's an awfully nice guy."

That attitude is a mistake. Inefficient labor shoots a small business down faster than almost anything else. Labor is usually a company's biggest expense. Small operators just don't have the margin to carry deadwood—not to mention that employees are usually the most prominent point of contact with customers.

If you are squeamish about firing people, then you will just have to get over it, that's all. When it becomes necessary, do it as quickly and cleanly as possible. The longer you wait, the harder it becomes. The job is easier if you don't mangle the worker's ego and pride. Instead of telling discharged employees not to let the door hit them on the way out, compliment them on a few things, even if you have to lie to do it. That makes the task more palatable. For example, tell them they have valuable attributes that would be more useful in another line of work. By helping them retain their dignity, the dirty deed transforms into something more humane.

Small business people must be wary of another problem when applying Japanese management methods. They must be careful of falling into the familiarity-breeds-contempt trap—that is, of letting employees get too close to them on a personal level. The chances of having an effective employer-employee relationship are lost once an employee becomes a personal friend. The danger of this happening is especially acute in small firms. The fewer the number of employees, the closer their interaction with management. Stay aloof. If you don't, your status as boss will evaporate. Some people are natural-born leaders whose very presence commands respect. If you are one of these, congratulations. If not, then avoid chumminess with employees. Insist on a certain amount of formality. That way, if employees can't respect you as a person, at least they can respect the uniform you are wearing.

When hiring, always require applicants to submit written résumés describing their background and job history, and giving references. Be sure to check with previous employers. Take what you are told with a grain of salt because former employers seldom really level with you. As Robert Half likes to say, "A bad reference is as hard to find as a good employee." In today's sue-happy environment, bosses avoid bad-mouthing former employees. Who wants a defamation of character suit? I know of instances in which embezzlers were recommended by the very employers from whom they embezzled. Their previous employers wanted them to find new jobs so they could earn enough money to pay back what had been stolen from them!

Despite the reluctance of most references to be forthright, seek them out anyway. You can usually pick up clues and inferences by talking to former bosses, and you should be able to uncover the fact that a prospective employee is a real ding-a-ling if you talk to enough people.

Employment agencies can be useful in preliminarily screening applicants, but don't depend on them too much. An employment agency's judgment is distorted by its eagerness for placement fees. Agencies usually do very little actual checking into an applicant's background.

It costs only $100 or so to have a background check and urine test done on a prospective employee. Do it. Screening out drug users and people with undisclosed criminal records will save you many times over the cost.

Never chew out an employee in front of other employees, even if he or she has it coming. Nothing is more destructive to a person's ego than being humiliated in front of peers. Don't criticize the worker in public, either. A verbal undressing while the whole world watches eliminates whatever chance you ever had of developing the person into an effective employee. In addition, berating someone in front of others makes you look like a Captain Queeg–type petty tyrant. Instead, chew out the culprit in private.

Be very, very careful who your customers are exposed to. Nothing kills goodwill quicker than having customers handled by abrasive, gum-chewing, "I-don't-know-I-just-work-here" employees. The most important person in the world is your customer. Ironically, lower-level employees are often the only ones customers ever come in contact with. So, for heaven's sake, make sure employees are adequately trained in customer relations.

One of America's most successful department store chains has an inverted organization chart. It is an upside-down pyramid. Customers are at the top of its organization chart instead of company officials. The next level of command on the chart consists of lower-level sales clerks, the people actually serving the customers. Only after those two levels does the regular company hierarchy start to appear.

I'm skeptical of non-monetary fringe benefits. Fringes are nice but money is nicer. Most employees are oriented toward near-term gratification. They tend to be radically predisposed toward the present. This is why employees relate to compensation much more if it is in the form of cold, hard cash. There is no substitute for what the long green stuff provides. So deferred bonuses and retirement plans aren't nearly as effective as monthly cash bonuses. Always remember, an inverse relationship exists between time and incentive. Bonuses payable 12 months in the future are worth one twelfth of bonuses paid each month, even though the total dollars are the same.

You would be amazed at how effective bonuses can be if they are tied directly to individual performance. But there has to be a recognizable link between the bonus and the activities of the recipient, such as the number of feet of pipe laid, or the squares of plasterboard put up, or the amount of undamaged parts produced. Many companies have a hard time establishing a conveniently measurable connection, but you should try to find one if you can. Then tie compensation to it. The productivity enhancement will startle you.

A common pitfall that many employers free-fall into is offering key employees small ownerships in the business as extra compensation. The share offered is not enough to impact the owner's control, mind you, but it is enough to represent that the employee has a piece of the rock. The thought is noble. Giving, say, one percent of your stock to key employees should inculcate them with entrepreneurial incentives, or so the reasoning goes. By owning stock, albeit tiny percentages, the anointed should be transformed into owner-type mentalities.

Friends, it doesn't work that way! Every time I've seen small business people try it, it has backfired. What's an employee going to do with one percent of a small, closely held company? Eat the stock certificate? The employee can't buy anything with it either. So what good is it, other than to hang on the wall as a conversation piece? Employees quickly come to realize one percent ownership doesn't give them anything in terms of real say or power. And they know the company retains earnings for expansion rather than paying out dividends to stockholders.

But, say you, someday the company may be worth big bucks and may be sold, or even may go public. Forget it. That's far in the distant future, not to mention being highly speculative. So the employees become disgruntled, cynical minority investors and the owner winds up buying back their stock to get them out of his or her hair. Always remember: A reward must be imminent if it is going to be a true incentive booster.

There is one secret to being an employer that is late in coming for most people. That is this: The perfect employee doesn't exist. The perfect employee is a mythological creature, a two-legged unicorn. All employees have strengths and weaknesses simply because they are members of the human race. What you must do is find a way to use their strengths while working around their weaknesses.

For example, suppose you have some old dragon on the payroll who is one hell of a worker but is abrasive and prone to fight with whomever he or she meets. You are impressed by this person's ability but are sick and tired of the squabbles and hassles he or she generates. The solution is simple. Isolation. Stick the problem employee in a separate office and channel everything through you. The point is, don't be adverse to working out individualized accommodations to take advantage of an employee's strong points. You have to be tolerant of a certain amount of idiosyncrasies. After all, you must have some yourself or else you wouldn't be an entrepreneur.

The best strategy for small business people, though, is to be very particular when it comes to choosing employees. The negative influence of a bad employee is much greater in a small work force than in a large one. Here is a list of some employee types you should try to avoid:

- Applicants whose employment history includes many previous jobs of short duration. Invariably there is some kind of personality problem.

- Applicants who are overqualified for the position. There's too much of a chance they'll use you as a temporary stopover while waiting for their ship to come in.

- Applicants preoccupied with time-consuming hobbies or outside activities. People with some kind of really big thing or cause in their life don't make stable employees.

- Applicants who are relatives. Nepotism is an insidious trap. Relatives usually turn out to be either bad employees or very bad employees. And they are four times as hard to get rid of as a nonrelative employee. Establishing an effective employer-employee relationship is difficult enough as it is without having to deal with the employee being your sister's snot-nosed only son.

Finally, I must mention a disagreeable subject—the law. Not being a man of the bar, I'm not qualified to spout legal advice. But there are some basic employee-related legal concepts with which you should have passing familiarity. Besides the IRS, there are three federal agencies and their applicable state counterparts you should avoid running afoul of. These are the Equal Employment Opportunity Commission (EEOC), Occupational Safety and Health Agency (OSHA), and the Department of Labor.

These agencies are as ominous as they sound. Those of our clients who have dealt with them have lived to regret it. They have found them intractable, biased, unsympathetic to employer problems, and, in general, the epitome of bureaucratic nightmares. This is what these agencies are all about:

EEOC administers the federal Civil Rights Act, which prohibits employer-related discrimination with regard to age; sex; marital status; race; creed; color; national origin; and sensory, mental, or physical handicaps. You can browbeat people all you want as to actual performance on the job, but your considerations and evaluations can't involve any of the sacred cow attributes mentioned in the Civil Rights Act. The act applies to any business that has 15 or more employees, that has federal contracts, or that works on federally funded construction contracts.

Even if you fall outside of those requirements, you still may be subject to antidiscrimination rules, because most states have similar laws applicable to smaller companies. For example, my home state (Washington) has laws that mimic the federal act applying to businesses with as few as eight employees.

Unfortunately, regardless of how frivolous or groundless an employee's discrimination complaint may be, it is time-consuming and stressful to deal with the agency handling the complaint. Civil rights violation hearings tend to resemble kangaroo courts and often require legal representation.

The best defense is documentation, documentation, and more documentation. Create written records of all dealings with employees and keep big, thick personnel files on them. The point is, the burden of proof, for practical purposes, is on you. Being the employer, you may be called upon to justify decisions regarding workers that seemed perfectly innocent at the time made. But without notes and correspondence that evidence what was going on back then, how do you prove your word against that of a noisy, complaining employee?

OSHA represents federal laws prescribing workplace standards for employee health and safety. State laws and agencies carry out these requirements. The feds only get involved if state laws are administered too loosely. OSHA standards are very extensive and detailed.

Government officials may initiate inspections at the company facility or on job sites. In addition, company employees can file OSHA violation complaints anonymously. It goes without saying that you as a decent human being want to provide a safe work environment. But OSHA rules can be picayunish and often represent overkill. Be sure you are familiar with at least the most basic workplace rules and standards. State agencies often provide a free consulting service for employers whereby violations can be pointed out on a penalty-free basis before the agency gets around to a formal inspection.

The U.S. Department of Labor administers laws governing basic employee rights. Most states have similar overlapping laws. Common rules (which can vary depending upon the state) cover such things as:

1. Minimum wages

2. Time-and-a-half pay for overtime (more than 40 hours worked per week)

3. Meal and rest periods (30-minute meal period for stretches of work over five hours, and 10-minute rest periods for every four hours worked)

4. Maternity leaves of absence, with the same or similar job at the same pay upon return

Normally, these don't apply to executives, professional employees, outside sales persons, some small retail and service businesses, or farm workers.

We have gone from the Age of Aquarius to the Age of the Petty Bureaucrat. Irony of ironies. In the name of humanity, our social laws have created inhuman instruments of implementation—faceless, amorphous bureaucracies.

Even though you are a small-fry business, you are still subject to an incredible array of inflexible rules and regulations. More than you can possibly keep track of. As a result, even if you try your best to comply, a peevish, spiteful, disgruntled employee can cause you grief. All he or she has to do is file complaints with the appropriate authorities. Whether real or imagined, you must dance while implacable bureaucrats shoot bullets at your feet.

This is one more argument for treating employees as sensitive human beings rather than pieces of meat. It may sound as if we are discussing blackmail here, but the best policy is not to ruffle the emotional feathers of employees too much. Deal with them in a businesslike and professional manner and try not to let your subjective feelings show. Have reasonable rationales for decisions regarding employees, and accumulate documentation in the form of notes and correspondence to back up your judgments.

Let me offer one final thought that overlays everything we've discussed. When dealing with employees, always keep one thing in mind: The average person gets slugged with 1,000 put-downs throughout his or her life for every pat on the back received. So always remember: Pass out a compliment now and then. It will pay bigger dividends in terms of employer-employee relations than anything else you can possibly do.

CHAPTER 35

SOLVING PAPERWORK GRIDLOCK

We can lick gravity, but sometimes the paperwork is overwhelming. Werner von Braun, rocket scientist

The paperwork involved in running a small business is incredible. Here are some of the forms and government reports the typical small business person gets tangled up with. (Relax. I'm not asking you to memorize them; just scan the list.)

1. Federal income tax return

2. State income tax return

3. State business tax return

4. City business tax return

5. Federal employee payroll tax return

6. State unemployment tax return

7. Federal unemployment tax return

8. State industrial insurance report

9. Various federal and state payroll tax deposit forms

10. Annual state corporate license renewal

11. Quarterly estimated income tax payment forms

12. Federal Bureau of the Census report

13. Personal property tax affidavit

14. Annual Pension Plan reports—Form 5500

15. Union health and welfare reports (one for each union)

16. Federal employment of minorities report

17. Various information returns—Form 1099

18. Federal highway use tax return

19. Federal excise tax return

20. Employees' W-2 forms

21. Employees' W-4 forms

22. Non-highway use gas tax refund application

23. Form I-9, illegal alien verification

I've left some out, but this gives you the idea. In addition, there are bank statements, invoices, general correspondence, FAX messages, various bookkeeping journals, time-keeping records, purchase orders, copies of phone messages, accounting records, computer print-outs, inventory records, suppliers' statements, contracts, the corporate minute book, petty cash receipts, *ad nauseam, ad nauseam, ad nauseam*.

Just a few years of being in business creates a plethora of paperwork. How do you avoid being smothered by it all? Here are some hints:

Records Retention

It isn't necessary that paperwork be kept forever. Some of it, yes, but most can be thrown away after a few years. Only the following should be kept indefinitely:

General ledgers

Copies of income tax returns

Evidences of ownership, such as deeds, titles, rights-of-way, easement records, copyrights, patents, partnership agreements, and trademark registrations

Formal corporate documents, such as articles of incorporation, by-laws, minute books, and stock certificate records

Everything else, sooner or later, can be deep-sixed. The actual number of years a particular record should be kept depends upon the type of business you are in, the type of record it is, and your state's statute of limitations. The IRS has a three-year statute of limitations. However, it extends to six years if your gross income is understated by 25 percent or more. Consequently, most accounting records should be kept a minimum of six years. As to other records, check with your attorney. The important thing is to establish a timetable for disposal. Most people dutifully accumulate records year after year as though they were the Library of Congress. They can tell you how much pencils cost back in 1970, but their offices are so crowded they can't find the pencils they bought last week.

Filing

I wish I had a lottery ticket for every minute I've spent looking for misplaced or misfiled records. By now I'd have won the triple jackpot. The most logical filing system is alphabetical. But not everybody files alphabetically the same way. Suppose you receive a quotation on the price of parts for Job #101 from Mr. Smith, the sales manager of the Charles Jones Company. Do you file this under *Smith, Jones, Charles, Parts, Quotations, Job #101?*

It doesn't really matter as long as the category used is logical to you. Hence, don't give a clerk something to file without first marking on the document where you want it to go. If something might be useful and logical information under more than one category, make copies for duplicate filing. The extra time taken will save you in the long run.

Professional office experts recommend filing systems patterned after libraries. First establish broad categories; then establish subcategories within the broad categories; then alphabetize within the subcategories. For example, a broad category might be *Sales.* A subcategory within *Sales* might be *Complaints.* A complaint letter from Mrs. Paininthe-neck would be filed in this order: Sales, Complaints, then *P* for Paininttheneck.

Whole-Dollar Accounting

When was the last time you bothered picking up a penny lying on the ground? When was the last time you bought something with a penny? Pennies are worthless. They are so worthless it isn't worthwhile keeping track of them anymore. So round off all bookkeeping entries to the nearest dollar. Excluding the cents won't materially affect anything. Dollar rounding is permitted on all tax returns. Financial statements should be rounded even further—to the nearest hundred or thousand dollars.

Pareto's Law

You've never heard of Pareto's Law? Too bad, because it is a fundamental law of nature. However, you may intuitively be aware of its existence already. Pareto's Law is a family of frequency distribution curves describing situations in which significant items in a group are only a small part of the group's total population. Pareto's Law says that within any group, a few items are important and, relative to them, the rest are piddling.

For example, a small segment of the total population owns the biggest chunk of the country's wealth, a few members of any club carry on most of the club's activities, a small percentage of salespeople create the majority of a company's total sales, a few companies account for the lion's share of any particular industry, and only a small percentage of inventory items constitutes the bulk of an inventory's value. Pareto's Law can be usefully applied to the following:

ABC Inventory Control System   If you analyze your inventory, chances are you'll find something like the following:

A. Ten percent of the items equal 60 percent of its value.

B. Thirty percent of the items equal 30 percent of its value.

C. Sixty percent of the items equal 10 percent of its value.

Instead of keeping track of every single item in inventory, categorize the items according to the classifications above. Then account for your inventory using the following procedure:

"A items": Account for every individual item.

"B items": Keep track of the total and count individual items once in a while.

"C items": Estimate and count infrequently.

In other words, monitor big ticket items and don't waste your time on nuts and bolts.

Correlate customer traffic with company personnel. If you survey the number of customers going through your store throughout the day, you'll probably find peaks and valleys. If so, cut down on full-time employees and hire part-timers for the peak hours.

Test check vendors' invoices. Instead of checking every single bill you receive, check only those over a specific big dollar amount. Merely test check the smaller ones.

Trim your product line. Very likely a small number of products account for most of your company's sales. Consider eliminating the small movers. Concentrate on the big sellers instead.

One-Write Bookkeeping Systems

A one-write system is a hand-posted journal that makes multiple entries on several records by using carbon paper and a special pegboard. By creating several entries at one writing, bookkeeping time is reduced. One-write systems are the first step up from a straight manual posting system. They are particularly useful in recording payrolls and accounts receivable.

"Writ by Hand"

Instead of typing everything, you'll save considerable time if you write checks, invoices, statements, and short correspondence in longhand. Many people balk at this for fear that handwritten documents will reflect badly on their image. Phooey. You are running a business, not a beauty contest. Some of the most important business people I know correspond with handwritten notes.

Multiple Voucher Checks

Two-part, three-copy voucher checks are a great paperwork saver. They look like this:

The bottom part of the check describes the nature of the payment and its accounting classification. The gimmick is there are two carbon copies. The original is the actual check given the payee. One of the copies is filed in numeric order, which eliminates the need for a checkbook and check register. The other copy is attached to the payee's invoice and is filed alphabetically.

With this system, you eliminate the necessity of posting check information on check stubs or cash disbursement journals, thus saving considerable bookkeeping time. Meanwhile, the invoice copy gives you a good record of when you paid the bill.

THE SECOND COMING OF THE WOOLLY MAMMOTH

Batch Your Work

Long production runs are more efficient than short runs. That's elementary. The trouble is, most small business people forget this basic fact of life during the confusion of running their daily affairs. Whenever possible, batch your work and have employees do the same. Stick with a job throughout its completion, or at least until you reach a logical stopping point.

Write and record checks at one time during the month rather than throughout the month. Do your invoicing at one time, post accounts receivable at one time, do your filing at one time, do correspondence at one time, and so on.

Delegate

As a small business owner, your most precious commodity is your own time. Be stingy with it. Don't squander it doing things employees can do for you. Learn to delegate.

Many small business people become overly fearful of potential mistakes their employees might make, so they wind up trying to cover all of the bases themselves. They become trapped by the if-you-want-it-done-right-do-it-yourself syndrome. It is better to tolerate a few bone-headed employee mistakes if this allows you to take care of the really important stuff. It should be self-evident that delegation of authority is the only way to go, unless you want to stay exceedingly small. Keep reminding yourself this is so.

The Paperwork Machine

Why, you might ask, haven't I mentioned computers as a paperwork saver? Computers don't save paperwork. They create paperwork. Reams and volumes and miles of it. Computers never create less of anything except less time to create more of everything, thereby requiring more time for more analysis of more reports and more understanding for more things and more storage for more paperwork. Computers are used because they do some things faster, better, and more efficiently—not because they cut down on paperwork.

Question Your Habits

Mark Twain once wrote, "We travel in ruts worn deep by time and custom. He who would change their path is undertaking a long project." We are all creatures of habit. It is good every once in a while to ask yourself soul-searching questions like the following: Why am I doing this? What does it accomplish? Why is it important? Can it be done better? Is there a shortcut? Can it be simplified? Would it cost less if it were done by someone else? Are there more important things to be done? Do I have all the facts? Am I being realistic? Is this making me any money? Will it make me money in the future? In short, it's a good idea to question your actions, ideas, objectives, and habits.

CHAPTER 36

WHAT TAXES ARE REALLY ALL ABOUT

It is not true that Congress spends money like a drunken sailor. Drunken sailors spend their own money. Congress spends our *money.*   Arthur Laffer

If Pandora's Box really existed, it would contain our income tax laws. The Internal Revenue Code and Regulations are so complicated I don't even want to bring up the subject. Nothing very meaningful can be portrayed in the brief time at my disposal. Nevertheless, something needs to be said, because taxes are an important consideration in small business.

Most people new to business have a distorted picture of taxes. When someone comes into my office to discuss going into business for themselves, invariably they make a sly comment along the lines of, "Now I can write off my car and house and club dues and claim all of those business deductions (wink, wink)." Whereupon I immediately reach for my balloon-popping needle and set about putting the fellow straight. One of the most persistent misconceptions in American business mythology is the idea that, once you own a business, everything from that point on automatically becomes deductible. Business people don't pay taxes, only non-business people pay taxes, right?

The fact is, Congress and the IRS have worked hand-in-hand for the past 25 years to close tax loopholes and clamp down on tax gimmicks. So it is a misbegotten perception that being in business constitutes a tax windfall.

There used to be a time when it was possible to "sneak" quasi-personal expenses through the tax return of a business. And it used to be that certain fringe benefits were available to owners of business corporations. However, the actual magnitude of those tax breaks was grossly exaggerated in the minds of the general public. And what wasn't an exaggeration has long since been eliminated by Congress.

But some myths die hard. The common perception still exists that owning a business means you are entitled to have Uncle Sam pay for your yacht and the costs of serving refreshments on board to your buddies. Business entertaining is deductible, right? Yes, but *not* if it involves an entertainment facility such as a yacht or a ski lodge, and not if it is goodwill entertaining without substantial and bona fide business discussions, and not if it isn't ordinary and necessary, and not if it doesn't reasonably relate to your trade or business.

Explaining to a new client that being in business doesn't automatically make everything under the sun deductible is always an uncomfortable task. The client invariably looks like a kid who's just been told there is no Santa Claus. The first reaction is disbelief, because it contradicts a long-standing concept of things. So the client challenges the veracity of my correcting statements: "Whadda-ya mean? I was talking to a friend of mine whose brother-in-law's been in business for years and he says he writes off all kinds of stuff like that." Or he might say, "Whadda-ya mean? Joe Blow told me he deducts all his Mystic Knights of the Sea Lodge dues and bar bills."

It took me a while to develop a diplomatic response to second-, third-, and fourth-hand gossip of this nature. After all, you don't want to start off insulting a new client or appear patronizing or condescending. So I gently remind the client that business people bragging about tax deductions is like teenage boys discussing their sex lives. Both grossly exaggerate. Of course, instances do exist where people get away with deductions they aren't entitled to simply because the IRS hasn't caught up with them. Due to increased sophistication of IRS computer programs, this is becoming less common, but it still happens.

Having said all of that, I must now tell you there are some legitimate tax benefits associated with being in business. Most are aimed at making it easier for small businesses to grow and stay within the owner's family. For that reason, they are not especially exotic or glamorous, but they do exist and it is important that you are aware of them since they can have long-range impact on a closely held business.

For example, there is an important tax advantage taking effect when you die. If a small business owner croaks and the value of the business constitutes a substantial part of the owner's estate, estate tax pertaining to the value of the business can be paid in installments over 14 years at favorable interest rates as long as the estate retains control of the business. In addition, if other family members own portions of the company at the time of the owner's death, a low value for estate tax purposes can often be established because of lack of a ready resale market for partial interests in a closely held business.

Probably the most important tax consideration for small businesses has to do with whether to incorporate. From a tax standpoint, incorporation is a many-handed proposition. On the one hand, corporate tax at lower income levels can be less than what the owner would pay as an individual. On the other hand, profits of corporations are potentially taxed twice—once at the corporate level and once again if extracted as dividends by the stockholders. On the other-other hand, double taxation of corporate profits may be of no practical significance under some circumstances. Then, on that other hand over there, corporate tax can be more than individual tax if income gets too high.

Here is what I am talking about. Corporate tax rates are 15 percent on the first $50,000 of taxable income (except for "personal service" corporations—doctors, lawyers, engineers, CPAs, and so on—whose corporations are taxed at a flat 34 percent rate). Individuals (married, joint return) leave the 15 percent bracket after reaching income in the mid-$30,000 range. Corporate tax is 25 percent on the next $25,000 of income, whereas married individuals pay at 28 percent. The cross-over point is $75,000, because corporate income from that point on is taxed at higher rates than individual income.

Suppose the net income of a business is $100,000. Suppose, further, that the owner draws out one half of the profit ($50,000) and reinvests the other half in the business. By incorporating, the owner would save over $7,000 of income tax and social security tax, at current rates. If those annual tax savings were invested at six percent, they would grow to $100,000 in 10 years! When's the last time you made $100,000 by merely buying a license from the state?

On the other hand, if the net income of the business is $500,000 and the owner draws out $200,000, the owner would save over $9,000 per year by *not* incorporating. The point is, corporate rates are an advantage only for little guys.

Furthermore, the advantage exists only if profits are left within the corporation. Obviously, lower rates are lost once income is extracted as bonuses or dividends. Usually, this is no problem. Small businesses normally have to retain most of their earnings to repay borrowings and to fund future expansion.

Ultimately, though, the time comes to "pay the piper." Profits retained by the corporation will be taxed again if stockholders take them out in the future. Suppose the owner retires or decides to sell the corporation? Accumulated profits of the corporation will have been taxed previously at the corporate level. Now the owner gets taxed again on those same profits when he or she receives the proceeds from a liquidation or sale. The same is true if he or she removes them as dividends.

But it gets even worse than that. If the owner tries to cash in the chips by liquidating the corporation, the corporation will have to pay tax on any unrealized increase in value contained in its assets. For example, suppose the corporation owns a building it purchased years ago for $250,000. Today, its book value is only $50,000 because of depreciation write-offs, but its real value is $1,000,000.

The owner decides to retire but wants to hang on to the building as an investment. Liquidating the corporation will cause the owner to pay tax on the building's $1,000,000 value. That's bad enough, but the corporation will also pay tax on the same $1,000,000 even though nothing was sold. All that really happened is that title was transferred to the stockholder who already indirectly owned the building because of owning the corporation. Yet, based upon the described facts, it is Disaster City because it triggers a combined liquidation tax of $500,000. This is known as The General Utilities Rule and was created by the so-called 1986 Tax Reform Act.

Okay, how about selling the corporation itself? Can't we escape double tax that way? Nice try, but no cigar. The owner still pays tax on the corporation's retained profits because they are part of its sale price. In addition, the purchaser will want a stepped-up tax basis in the corporation's assets, but the only way the purchaser can get this is to have the corporation pay what amounts to a general utilities tax on the assets' value. Naturally, the purchaser will pass that expense on to the former owner by deducting it from the amount that he or she is willing to pay for the corporation.

Mitigating double tax of corporate earnings is the lower corporate tax rate applicable at lower income levels. To the extent this applies, there is interest-free use of deferred tax dollars for the intervening years. Also, if the owner doesn't sell, he or she may be able to take accumulated profits out as additional salary or bonus, which, although taxable to the owner, is deductible to the corporation.

There is one way a corporation can be utilized without incurring double tax, although the tax advantage of corporate rates is lost: File an election with the IRS to have your company taxed as an "S" corporation. For tax-reporting purposes, an "S" corporation is treated essentially the same as a partnership or a sole proprietorship. "S" corporations don't pay tax themselves (except under special circumstances), because their taxable income or loss is reported on the stockholders' individual returns. However, there are many technical requirements for "S" status as well as some tax traps involved, so you will need to discuss the subject with a qualified tax expert before initiating an "S" election.

It used to be that one main reason (tax-wise) to incorporate was the superiority of corporate pension and profit-sharing plans over unincorporated plans. However, Congress has since passed legislation making non-corporate retirement plans on a par with corporate plans—except for one aspect. For some unexplained reason, corporate owners are allowed to borrow from their pension plan accounts, whereas pension plans of unincorporated businesses are severely restricted from loaning to owners. This feature continues to make corporate plans somewhat superior.

One special form of corporate retirement plan does have a unique tax advantage. Employee Stock Option Plans (ESOPs) are corporate pension plans set up to invest in the company's own stock instead of in outside investments. When a business owner retires under an ESOP plan, he or she can sell the stock back to employees through the plan and defer tax on the redemption as long as he or she reinvests the proceeds in another corporation. Do you see the possibilities? Under an ESOP plan, a retiring business owner can transform the company's value into stock of a large publicly held company and not pay tax on the transaction. Any drawbacks? You didn't think the god of There's-No-Free-Lunch would let you off that easy, did you? In order to get yourself in this position, you must dilute your ownership ahead of time by giving employees a substantial interest in your business through company contributions to the ESOP.

There are potential tax traps associated with corporations. These traps involve situations in which the business is no longer active and the owner converts the business assets into passive investments. Under this scenario, there is danger the corporation may turn into (horror of horrors) something called a "personal holding company." Or, what is worse, it may fall prey to the dreaded "accumulated earnings tax." Or perhaps it may blunder inadvertently into the fiendish "collapsible corporation" trap. These categories generate special tax penalties. In other words, when a business owner wishes to retire, he or she may find that most investments are locked up within the corporation, and the only way they can be accessed is to dissolve the corporation and pay a stiff liquidation tax.

There are also potential tax pitfalls associated with the ongoing operation of a corporation. These mostly arise when a business loses money. A common trap is to have tax losses frozen within the corporation where they cannot be utilized by the owners personally. There are methods of passing corporate tax losses on to stockholders through such things as the previously mentioned "S" election as well as the small business stock loss provisions of Section 1244. But these require keen awareness and astute tax advice.

All in all, operating a small business is neither a tax bonanza nor a tax burden. As in all other areas of business endeavor, it requires proper planning and common sense. Finally, be aware that a big element of subjectivity exists in tax matters, because much of the Tax Code and Regulations is general in nature even though taxpayers must deal in specifics. The difference in frame of reference causes many disputes between taxpayers and the IRS, which, in turn, causes thousands of tax court cases every year handing down interpretations and clarifications. This means you can't always be too sure ahead of time of the answer to a tax question.

A recent tax court case (*Blackman* vs. *Commissioner*) illustrates this. The taxpayer had a rip-roaring argument with his wife and, in a fit of pique, set fire to some of her clothes on the kitchen stove. The fire got out of control and burned the whole house down, plus its contents. The taxpayer's insurance company refused to pay the claim because the fire was caused by the taxpayer. Hoping to salvage something out of a disastrous situation, the taxpayer claimed a casualty loss deduction on his tax return. The IRS disallowed the deduction, even though it technically satisfied the code's definition. The tax court agreed with the IRS, saying that allowing the deduction would frustrate public policy against using fire to settle domestic disputes!

Here's a tax-planning suggestion. If he had eaten his wife's clothes instead of burning them, perhaps he would have qualified for a medical expense deduction.

Iteration: *A method of solving problems by trial and error through repeated application of successive approximations, each building on the one preceding until accuracy is achieved.* Antonym: *Life itself, which for most of us is one long trial by erroneous application of unsuccessful approximations.*

CHAPTER 37

ALICE IN TAXLAND

(UNABRIDGED VERSION)

Trying to explain complex tax rules in a way that is halfway comprehensible has me stumped. Particularly passive activity rules, which apply to people investing in small business "S" corporations and partnerships. It might help if Alice took us by the hand and walked us through the looking glass. We find ourselves suddenly in the middle of Taxland, surrounded by all of those familiar characters—Tweedledum, Tweedledee, the Queen of Hearts, the Cheshire Cat, the White Rabbit—they are all there. Imagine they are the ones doing the explaining.

"There are two kinds of losses," said the Queen. "Good losses and bad losses."

"What do you mean by that?" asked the Caterpillar, puffing on his hookah. "I thought all losses were bad?"

"Don't be impertinent!" said the Queen. "Good losses can be deducted against other income. Bad losses can only be deducted against themselves. They are called PALs."

"How can you deduct a loss against itself?" asked Alice, "And if they are 'bad' losses, why are they called PALs?"

"Ah, that's a great puzzle," said the Mad Hatter, as he poured himself another cup of tea.

"You don't know much, and that's a fact," said the Duchess. "*PAL* stands for 'passive activity loss.'"

"Of course, sometimes a PAL can turn into a PIG, and vice-versa," said the Cheshire Cat, who kept fading in and out of view. "Then you can deduct the losses you weren't able to deduct before. Unless, of course, you give the activity away first," he said, fading away gradually. "Or, unless you die second," echoed his grin.

"Since you don't know very much, I suppose I'll have to tell you *PIG* stands for 'passive income generator,'" said the Duchess, barely bothering to hide her annoyance.

"Do I have to wait for a PAL to turn into a PIG, or can I deduct a passive activity loss against a different activity's passive income?" said Alice, feeling quite proud of herself for thinking of such a smart question to ask.

"Naturally," said the Duchess, "unless, of course, it is passive income generated by a publicly traded partnership."

"What is a publicly traded partnership?" asked Alice.

"Ah. That's a great puzzle," said the Mad Hatter, pouring his tea on the Dormouse.

"Furthermore," said Alice, "what is a passive activity to begin with, anyway?"

"Well put," said the Caterpillar. "It is always best to begin the beginning at the beginning. That's what I always say," as he choked conspicuously on his hookah.

"A passive activity is a trade or business you don't materially participate in," said the Queen, sonorously. "Everyone knows that. It's right here in *The Regulations*," pointing her scepter at a big, thick, ominous-looking book.

"Unless, of course, it is a rental activity," interjected the Cheshire Cat, who had just materialized back into view. "Then it is passive activity, all the same."

"Except if the rental is real estate," said the March Hare, "in which case you get a $25,000 loss deduction."

"Unless your adjusted gross income exceeds $100,000," piped up the White Rabbit, "in which case the $25,000 deduction is reduced by 50 cents on the dollar."

"Or, unless you don't 'actively' participate in the real estate rental or don't own at least 10 percent," interjected the Dormouse.

"Don't forget," chimed in the Walrus, "working interests in oil and gas properties are active even if you are passive."

"Unless, of course, you are a limited partner," chipped in the Mock Turtle.

"Nobody's mentioned the phase-in rule, yet," said the Unicorn. "Yes, yes. The phase-in rule," everyone shouted. In unison, they chanted:

"In 1987, POW! Thirty-five percent of PALs disallow. In '88, sorry Rube, 60 percent goes down the tube. In '89, look out, Jack, 80 percent you won't get back. In 1990, whadda-ya know, Bill, 90 percent goes over the hill. In '91, what a crime, 100 percent isn't worth a dime!"

"Unless, of course, they are activities that were acquired after October 22, 1986, in which case the phase-in rules don't apply," cautioned the White Rabbit, after everyone else was quiet.

"And unless, of course, you are computing the alternate minimum tax," squeaked the Dormouse.

"Don't mention that word!" thundered the Queen. "That is the subject of another chapter!" The Dormouse crept back into the teapot and everyone grew silent again.

"I'm so confused," said Alice. "You haven't explained what 'materially participate' means."

"Idiot!" said the Queen. "I already told you, it's in *The Regulations*. Read *The Regulations!*" she commanded, turning to the Knave of Hearts.

After considerable hacking, coughing, and throat clearing, the Knave of Hearts read:

"Ahem. Material participation: A taxpayer who is not a limited partner (or who owns a general partnership interest in addition to a limited partner interest during the partnership tax year ending within the partner's tax year) is a material participant in an activity during the tax year if he or she meets one of the following tests: (1) participates in the activity for more than 500 hours, or (2) provides substantially all of the participation conducted in the activity conducted by individuals (including non-owners), or (3) participates more than 100 hours and no other individual's participation in the activity exceeds that of the taxpayer, or (4) the activity is a significant participation activity (see below) for the tax year and the taxpayer's total participation in all significant participation activities for the year exceeds 500 hours, or . . .

(pant, pant)

. . . the taxpayer has materially participated in the activity for any five of the 10 preceding years, consecutively or nonconsecutively, as the case may be, or (6) the activity is a personal service activity [see paragraph 1.469-5T(d)] in which the taxpayer has materially participated for any three preceding tax years, or (7) in light of all the facts and circumstances, the taxpayer participates in the activity on a regular, continuous, and substantial basis and spends at least 100 hours in the activity . . .

(gasp, gasp)

Limited partners materially participate in an activity only if they meet one of tests (1), (5), or (6) above."

(The Knave of Hearts collapses on the ground, completely out of breath. He is revived by the Mad Hatter, who pours tea on his head.)

"I don't agree with the 'facts and circumstance' test," commented Tweedledum. "If it is a fact, then it must be so, but if it is also a circumstance, then it must not be a fact, for how can it be both?, and if it isn't a fact, then it might not be so, unless, perhaps, it is a fact that it is circumstantial, or, maybe circumstantially a factuality, on the other hand, if . . ."

"Shut up!" snapped the Queen, and everyone looked nervous.

"It appears to me it is important not to be called a rental activity," said Alice. "Otherwise, you become a passive activity, even if you go to the bother of being a material participant."

"Quite so, my dear," said the Queen, condescendingly.

"When is an activity a 'rental activity,' then?" asked Alice.

"It's in *The Regulations!*" boomed the Queen. "Read from *The Regulations!*" she said, turning once again to the poor Knave of Hearts.

Wearily staggering to his feet and brushing tea leaves from his jacket, the Knave of Hearts read:

"Subject to certain major exceptions (see below), in general, an activity is rental activity for a tax year if: (1) during the tax year, tangible property held in connection with the activity is used by customers or is held for use by customers, and (2) the gross income attributable to the conduct of the activity during the tax year represents amounts paid principally for the use of the tangible property. . . .

(puff, puff)

"Major exceptions referred to above are as follows: (1) the average period of customer use is seven days or less (see below), or (2) the average period of customer use is 30 days or less, and significant personal services (see below) are provided by the owner, or on behalf of the owner, in connection with making the property available for use, or (3) without regard to the period of customer use, extraordinary personal services (see below) are provided by or on behalf of the owner or in connection with making the property available for use by the customer, or . . .

(wheeze, wheeze)

". . . (4) the rental is treated as incidental to a non-rental activity, or (5) the property is customarily made available during defined business hours for the nonexclusive use of customers, or (6) the taxpayer provides property for use in an activity that is conducted by a partnership, "S" corporation or joint venture in which he or she owns an interest, and the activity is not a rental activity. . . .

(hyperventilate, hyperventilate)

"Significant personal services, referred to above for purposes of the second factor noted above, means services performed by individuals but does not include the following excluded services: (1) services necessary to permit lawful use of the property, and (2) services in the nature of permanent improvements or repairs that substantially extend the property's life beyond normal customer use, and (3) services performed in connection with the use of real property that are similar to those commonly provided in connection with long-term rentals of high-grade commercial or residential real property, but . . .

(gurgle, gurgle)

". . . in determining whether personal services are significant, all relevant facts and circumstances are to be taken into account. Extraordinary personal services, referred to above for purposes of item (3) above are provided only if provided by individuals and the customer's attendant use of the subject property is incidental to receiving those services."

By now, the poor Knave of Hearts was obviously in distress, but he valiantly continued on:

"Average period of customer use, referred to above, for a particular tax year, is determined by dividing (1) the aggregate number of days in all periods of customer use for the property that end during the tax year, by (2) the number of the periods of customer use, but, for purposes of this formula, each period during which a customer has continuous or recurring right to use an item of property that is held in connection with the activities is treated as a separate period of customer use and this rule applies without regard to whether the customer uses the property for the entire period or whether the right to use the property is under one agreement or renewals of the agreement."

The Knave of Hearts expelled so much air reiterating all of this that he collapsed like a limp rag into the teapot, much to the Mad Hatter's disgust.

"I don't agree with all the 'see belows' and 'referred to aboves,'" said Tweedledee. "If you are seeing below and at the same time looking above, you can't keep track of anything, except, maybe, where you once were, assuming you weren't already halfway in between, or perhaps where you would be or maybe where you used to be, or possibly are about to be, or perhaps, unless of course, you . . ."

"Shut up!" raged the Queen. "I told you, it's in *The Regulations!* That's all you need to know, now or ever, above, below, sideways, inside out, upside-down or outside in!" Everyone looked nervous again.

By now, Alice was growing impatient. "This is such an odd place," she said, petulantly. "The more questions I ask, the curiouser and curiouser the answers become."

"That's because we are all mad here," said the Cheshire Cat's grin. "And we're mad because we all come from a mad place."

"Where is that?" asked Alice.

In chorus: "Congress! Do you know what we do there?" Whereupon the assemblage formed a big, nondescript, dancing circle and burst forth into a chant:

> Twas brillig, and the slithy toves
> Did gyre and gimble in the wabe,
> All mimsy were the borogoves,
> And the mome raths outgrabe.
> Beware the TaxLawWriter, my son!
> The words that obfuscate,
> The tax traps that catch!
> Beware the DumDumTaxCourt, and shun
> The frumious BanderSnatchTaxForms!

But Alice wasn't about to listen anymore. Covering her ears, she dashed back through the looking glass, hotly pursued by ten tax attorneys, fifteen CPAs, and one H&R Block franchise.

That concludes our tax lesson for today, children.

CHAPTER 38

DEALING WITH FINANCIAL TROUBLE

Sooner or later comes that humiliating, ignominious day when you add up your bills and discover you are short. There isn't enough money to pay everyone and you've already borrowed up to your eyeballs at the bank. Obviously, someone has to wait. Who don't you pay first?

First of all, pay no attention to the noises emanating from your creditors. Calm down. Relax. Now, cold-bloodedly analyze your bills and classify them as to their relative importance. This determines who gets paid first. There are three rough categories to sort them into:

1. They-can-shut-your-water-off bills

2. They-can-make-it-uncomfortable-for-you bills

3. They-can-wait bills

Category 1, shut-your-water-off bills, includes those that must be paid just to keep your doors open. Utilities are a prime example. Water, power, and telephone companies will cut you off right now if you become delinquent.

Also in category 1 are federal payroll taxes withheld from employee wages. Ironically, payroll taxes are often one of the first things that cash-short business people get behind on. It's easy to do, because business owners have physical control over the money. The temptation to delay forking over withheld payroll tax money is strong when you still have it in your pocket. However, payroll taxes are one of the worst things to defer. The IRS collection department is a rough customer. They'll padlock your doors if you don't pay promptly. They can even pierce your corporate veil and go after you personally for nonpayment. Furthermore, the resultant penalties and interest charges are a nasty bit of business.

Usually, a few key suppliers or services come under the shut-your-water-off category. These are creditors you depend upon for items vital to your business—the ones furnishing key ingredients to whatever it is you sell. Somehow, you have to keep these and all other category 1 bills current.

Category 2, make-it-uncomfortable creditors, are those that can make you sweat but can't immediately put you out of business. Examples are one-shot suppliers, or suppliers of items obtainable from multiple sources. If they refuse to supply you, the same goods can be obtained elsewhere, perhaps after only a small delay. Unsecured bank loans come under this category. Banks will scream like a wounded eagle when you go delinquent, but they normally can be stalled for considerable periods of time before pulling your plug. As a matter of fact, if you get into them for a substantial amount, the bank may even make additional loans to ensure that you stay afloat out of fear of losing what they already are owed.

Category 2 types can usually be kept at bay by simply feeding them partial payments. This is an important technique. A creditor doesn't have to accept partial payments, but most will gratefully receive them. What makes creditors most nervous is not hearing from you at all. Silence is what turns collection departments on. Partial payments, on the other hand, let creditors know you are alive and well and still in town trying to pay them off. Throwing a few bones to creditors won't necessarily make them happy but usually will forestall formal collection procedures.

The tricky thing about partial payments is making sure all category 2 bills are treated the same, not just the ones giving you heat. Many debtors make the mistake of paying only those making loud squawking noises. The quiet ones they ignore. Then, all of a sudden, one of the polite, quiet category 2 creditors turns into a sleeping pitbull who wakes up and clamps down with a vengeance, maybe even forcing a bankruptcy. The best policy is to treat all members of category 2 equally.

Finally, there is category 3, the they-can-wait bills. These include the ones you can stiff for extended periods of time. Most small bills come under this heading, such as office supplies, dues, subscriptions, small repair bills, printing and cleaning bills, and other minor items. When a bill is small—say, under $100—it costs more to collect than the bill itself. Hence, small creditors tend to be long-suffering. Although not small dollarwise, legal and accounting bills are they-can-wait types. Attorneys and accountants can't repossess anything and normally are reluctant to sue debtor clients. Furthermore, if they refuse to service your account, one of their competitors can usually be found hungry enough or dumb enough to work for a kiss and a promise.

Property taxes commonly belong in category 3. In most states, you can be delinquent several years before foreclosure. In addition, most jurisdictions impose no personal liability. Nonpayment only results in a lien on the underlying property.

The strategy for nonpayment of bills (*crisis management* is the euphemistic term) is a matter of deciding which category each bill falls into. Take mortgage payments. Oftentimes you can stall a long time before having to catch up with delinquent mortgage payments. Mortgage companies are very prompt at sending hair-raising delinquent notices, but they usually are slow to initiate formal foreclosure proceedings. They are reluctant to foreclose because they don't really want the underlying property on their hands, particularly this day and age when environmental laws make property owners liable for pollution problems created by previous owners. Also, they aren't anxious to incur the time and costs connected with a foreclosure action.

Sometimes landlords will tolerate several months of late rent before getting hard-nosed. Evicting you may be expensive and a bother. Besides, you'll usually have one or two months' extra rent on deposit anyway as one of the original requirements of the lease.

One way unsecured creditors can be held at bay is to hint they are pushing you toward bankruptcy. That, generally, is the last thing they want to happen. Experienced unsecured creditors know by the time attorneys, accountants, administrators, and preferred and secured creditors get through picking your bankrupt bones, nothing will be left for them. Their chances of getting paid are usually better if they let you keep your doors open. As a matter of fact, major creditors sometimes defer a customer's old balance and continue supplying on a pay-as-you-go basis. The idea is that current sales earn them current profits and, at the same time, may enable the debtor-customer to earn enough to clean up the old balance.

You create settlement-minded creditors anytime you get them to believe there is a reasonable chance you will go under. The minimax principle of game theory takes hold: Settling for fifty cents on the dollar may not be the maximum recovery they can get, but it does represent the highest minimum they can lose. In other words, they would rather be assured of receiving 50 percent than to take a 50 percent chance of receiving all or nothing.

So don't hesitate to bad-mouth yourself when cornered by creditors. Most inexperienced debtors do just the opposite. They paint a rosy picture for creditors of how things are looking up and how they're making money again and how they should be able to make a payment real soon. Hoping, of course, to talk their way into a reprieve. A creditor's normal reaction is: "Look, Slick, if things are going so great, how come you aren't paying me anything? You must be paying somebody; how come it ain't me?" As a result, they squeeze all the harder for payment.

When trapped on the phone by a creditor, most novice debtors try to mollify their tormentors with such inanities as, "Oh, haven't we paid you yet? I'll tell the bookkeeper to cut you a check right away." Or, "Gee, I guess we lost your invoice. Can you send us a duplicate?" Or, "The person who ordered that is no longer with us, but I'll check into it right away." Or, "I could have sworn we'd already paid that. Well, we'll take care of it next month then."

Rank amateurism. Everyone except a hopelessly naive ninny knows it is bovine scatology. What the pros do is shut off the phone. They filter phone calls through a secretary and answer only those not from creditors. Talking to creditors before you are ready to talk to them is a waste of time. It merely adds to your emotional trauma. It's hard enough working one's way out of a short working capital position without being tormented by duns. Only talk to those creditors with whom you hope to arrange some kind of a deal, and only after you are composed and ready to negotiate.

If creditors do, by chance, get through, the quickest way to brush them off is to lay your cards, or lack thereof, on the table. Level with them and say flat out you don't have any money but intend to settle up as soon as possible. You don't know exactly when that will be but are doing the best you can. If they get persistent or abusive, tell them to go ahead and sue but that they won't get paid any sooner. For good measure, you might add that they can put you through bankruptcy if they want, if they are willing to settle for two cents on the dollar. Then hang up.

If things get too horrible, it may be time to pull the plug. In other words, bankruptcy. In a bankruptcy, creditors must either dump their loans or accept a small settlement. When I was growing up, bankruptcy had a terrible stigma attached to it, like flunking out of school. Nowadays, it has become rather commonplace. The idea of bankruptcy is to wipe the debtor's slate clean of a hopeless situation so he or she gets a fresh start. And it does seem to work that way. Most people I know who have gone through bankruptcy bounce right back into business again; after a bankruptcy exorcism, their credit seems almost as good as it ever was. As a matter of fact, many creditors look upon a bankrupt individual as a relatively "clean" credit risk. Bankruptcy reduces the chance of there being old debts ahead of theirs. In addition, the "bankruptee" has to wait five more years before declaring bankruptcy again.

Meanwhile, "Dudley Do-Right"—the stouthearted, honorable fellow who stubbornly refused to give up until every last creditor was paid off— stays behind the eight ball indefinitely. Even though Do-Right hung on and successfully repaid everyone, his credit rating will be no better than that of his bankrupt brother, Cut-and-Run. The fact that Do-Right toughed it out and paid everybody doesn't alter his credit record showing him being chronically delinquent and slow. The moral is: Don't look upon bankruptcy as a fate worse than death.

Furthermore, if your corporation goes down the tube, it doesn't necessarily mean you have to flush yourself at the same time. As a stockholder, you are only responsible for those corporate debts you have personally signed for. That is what the limited liability of corporations is all about, isn't it? Consequently, never guarantee or sign personally for corporate obligations unless you are absolutely forced to.

There are some exceptions to the corporate shield against liabilities. As previously mentioned, corporate officers can be held personally liable for withheld payroll taxes. Also, a corporation can't be used to defraud creditors. As a matter of fact, courts can ignore the corporate entity altogether if its affairs are too closely linked to the owner's personal finances.

Even if the sky does fall down and you are forced into individual bankruptcy, all is not lost. You are permitted to exclude a certain amount of personal assets from creditors. These vary from state to state, but, generally speaking, a bankrupt individual can keep a modest house equity, a car, personal effects, the tools of the person's trade, and a small amount of cash. However, some debts aren't extinguished by bankruptcy. These debts include taxes, alimony payments, and property obtained under false pretenses.

Most delinquent debtors react with mortification to their situation. They bumble and mumble and bow and scrape. The thing to remember is, don't panic. Stay cool. Many businesses, even big ones, get into a financial sticky wicket now and then. So don't worry about your reputation. It's just part of the business game. Like being tackled behind your own goal line for a safety.

Classify your debts in the order I suggest so you can take care of them according to their priority. If things get hopeless, don't be afraid to think the unthinkable (bankruptcy). After the smoke has cleared, sit down and try to figure out what went wrong. Then make sure you don't make the same mistakes twice. If you're going to get into financial trouble again, at least have enough class to think up a different way of doing it.

Out of Court Settlement   Charles Bragg

CHAPTER 39

HOW TO MAKE PEOPLE PAY YOU

THE MONEY THEY OWE

Something that initiates people quickly into the facts of business life is the discovery that it is damn hard sometimes to collect your accounts receivable. When half of your receivables are delinquent or slow, it puts a real crimp in cash flow. Especially if your net profit margin is only five percent.

Normally, the reason customers don't pay isn't that they don't have the money. Rather, it is because they don't have enough money to pay all their bills at the same time. Accordingly, they follow the squeaky wheel principle. They pay whomever is yelling the loudest. Creditors who don't yell get put at the bottom of their bill pile.

As a bill collector, your strategy must be just the opposite of that utilized when you yourself are in financial trouble. The secret is to yell loud and long and often: "When are you going to pay your bill? I thought you said you were going to mail me a check last week? I need payment immediately, if not sooner! Pay up now!"

Most people, unless they are basically mean, don't enjoy this sort of thing. Bill collecting is a distasteful but necessary activity. Not putting the bite on delinquent debtors dooms you to their same fate. Soon you too will have the financial shorts.

It's best to accompany dunning with threats. Threaten to put debtors on a cash-on-delivery (COD) basis, or cut them off unless they bring their accounts current, or turn them over to a collection agency. Of course, nobody likes to alienate customers. In the case of a large customer, you may be reluctant to get too hard-nosed for fear of losing future business. If so, the next best thing is to hit them with polite requests that are frequent. Squeak softly, but often. Nag, nag, nag!

The point is, don't depend on a delinquent debtor's conscience. Unless you harrass the person, you'll inevitably wind up waiting for hell to unfreeze their bill pile before you get paid.

So much for slow receivables. Then there is the other kind. The ones that not only are slow but are potentially bad debts. The best approach toward reducing bad debts is not to create them in the first place.

Credit policy is similar to the insurance business. It is a game of statistics. If you take chances, you are going to take losses. Institute liberal credit, personal check-cashing privileges, and soft collection policies, and you will have bad debts: the statistics demand it. Inexperienced business people invariably start out being much too liberal in granting credit, fearing they will lose hard-to-come-by sales. What they don't realize is that the loss of a sale merely means loss of a potential profit, whereas a bad debt means losing the cost of the merchandise as well, which is actual money out of pocket.

I am a strong believer in tough credit policies and originally was going to recommend that great care be taken when extending credit. However, nobody ever pays any attention to this sort of advice, so I'm not going to bother giving it. I know from personal experience that when you're scraping and scratching for business and a flaky customer dangles a dollar in front of your nose, nine times out of 10 you'll grab for it. Anxiety for new business overcomes doubts as to credit reliability. So you don't bother asking for credit references or having your bank run a credit check or asking for advance deposits or cash on delivery. Instead, you wait until a debt goes sour before you come to your senses.

For that reason, I am going to resist the temptation of saying that most bad-debt problems can be avoided by being discriminating at the time of sale. Instead, I am going to concentrate on how to collect shaky receivables once they have been created.

Fast action is the important thing. Keep in mind that delinquent customers owe other people besides you, so it's a matter of who gets to them first. If you wait too long to act, you'll wind up being stiffed every time.

Having a small company, you can't afford an in-house collection department, so you'll have to turn over bad receivables to an outside collection agency or an attorney. Collection agency fees cost between 25 and 50 percent of collections, depending upon the size and nature of the debt. Attorneys usually charge roughly the same, except they may want to be paid on an hourly basis if the debt is really of doubtful collectibility.

Collection agencies are a little more efficient than most attorneys because they have more practical experience chasing deadbeats. On the other hand, if the debt is large, you'll probably have to sue for it eventually; so you might as well sic your attorney on it at the outset, because he or she will become involved sooner or later anyway.

One of the quickest ways to collect is simply to garnish, or attach, the debtor's bank account. This isn't quite as easy as it sounds because, first of all, you have to know where the debtor's bank account is located. Also, the debtor can sue you for damages if he or she can prove it was a wrongful attachment. Finally, the tendency of courts is to restrict garnishments to situations in which there has been due process of law—in other words, after there has been a hearing.

It is also possible to garnish a debtor's salary if he or she is employed. Here again, the judicial trend has been to require a hearing before allowing the garnishment. In addition, most states exempt a portion of the debtor's salary even if the garnishment is valid. At any rate, this is a procedure you will have to let your attorney handle.

If you do take a debtor to court, winning a judgment still might not get you your money. All the judgment means is the court agrees it is a legitimate debt. Unfortunately, debtor prisons went out of style some time ago, so you can't have the bum thrown in jail for refusing to pay. If the debtor ignores the judgment, your only recourse is to institute a foreclosure action on his or her assets. You may have to haul the debtor back into court under supplemental proceedings to discover where his or her assets are located. Still, there are advantages to obtaining a judgment. It gives you the legal muscle to squeeze payment from the debtor, assuming he or she has something to squeeze.

As you can see, collecting overdue receivables is a problem because it costs time and money. All hard-core deadbeats know this. Some will use this knowledge against you in an attempt to compromise their debts. An experienced deadbeat may say, "Okay, tell you what—I'll pay you if you cut my bill in half. Otherwise, you'll have to sue me for it."

This is a sneaky but effective ploy. The debtor knows that you realize that, what with attorney's fees and all, one-half is all you'll get anyway if you sue. Besides, suing takes time. So many people confronted with this sort of proposal wind up compromising. I think it's best to call the deadbeat's bluff—assuming, that is, there's no legitimate beef over your bill. A lawsuit will cost the debtor money too, so if you stick to your guns, he or she probably will become anxious to settle somewhere short of actually going to court.

Another flaky trick is to send you a partial payment containing the statement, "Acceptance of this check constitutes payment in full." I've had conflicting opinions from attorneys as to the validity of such statements. To avoid hassles, it's probably best simply to return the check. Then there is the ploy of sending you an unsigned check. This, supposedly, buys the time it takes to return the check so the debtor can correct the "inadvertent" oversight.

Another maneuver on your part is to have delinquent customers sign interest-bearing promissory notes specifying they will bear the cost of any future collection costs. When such a note is signed, it automatically fixes the amount owed. This makes it easier to sue a debtor if he or she defaults. For this reason, experienced slow-pay artists are reluctant to sign promissory notes, but it is worth a try.

If you are a subcontractor, you can ensure payment from the general contractor by filing what is known as a "materialman's lien." This is a lien attaching to the property you are working on. Materialman liens have to be filed shortly after your work is completed (within 60 days, in many states), so prompt action is needed to avail yourself of this protection. Equipment manufacturers can secure lien rights by having customers sign a security agreement (often referred to as a UCC filing). After the security agreement is recorded, it causes the seller to be a secured creditor with regards to the debt. Liens are fraught with legal technicalities, so you should seek guidance from an attorney to utilize them.

You can reduce collection costs on small debts by suing the debtor in small claims court. Attorneys aren't allowed in small claims courts of most states. Plaintiffs and defendants represent themselves, so this causes proceedings to be rather informal. The amount you can sue for is limited to a maximum amount varying by state. Usually, it is no more than a few thousand dollars. Unfortunately, small claims courts have crowded calendars, so you may have to waste time waiting for a hearing.

Collecting money is a disagreeable task. It's an expense and a bother most neophyte business people aren't prepared for. Consequently, they don't realize how much of a hassle it can be. Regardless of its unpleasantness, it can't be ignored. After all, you aren't in the banking business. And always remember: Benign neglect doesn't make collection problems go away; it just lets more of them in the door.

CHAPTER 40

DODGING COMPETITION:

LESSONS FROM BUSINESS BIOLOGY I

"So, do you think you are executive material, Jack?"
"Do you mean, can I play hardball?"
"No, I mean, can you kiss ass?"
From the movie *Head Office*

I began this book portraying my change in careers from biology to business. It is only fitting that I end up reversing the process by looking at business from a biologist's perspective.

It makes one cringe to read the flak that poor old Charlie Darwin took back in the 1800s when he published his books *The Origin of the Species* and *The Descent of Man*. As Salman Rushdie knows, nothing inflames human passions more than imagined violation of religious beliefs. Advancing the idea that organisms evolve into new forms wasn't so bad, even though it contradicts the Book of Genesis. What blew people away was the concept that humans are subject to the same laws, which equates human beings with animals: "You mean my one-hundred-thousand-times-removed uncle is a monkey? Blasphemy!" This is an objection that persists even today in the Bible Belt of our country.

However, despite isolated pockets of contrary belief, Darwin's ideas permeate scientific thought and are deeply ingrained in our culture. Like many important concepts, Darwin's theories have been used as a foundation for philosophical and social views, even though such notions go far beyond the original concept.

One group responding early on with sympathetic chord was the world of free enterprise. Entrepreneurs instinctively recognized parallelisms to belief in rough-and-tumble, no-holds-barred commercial competition. Evolution through natural selection fits well with philosophic homilies such as "survival of the fittest," "the law of the jungle," "nice guys finish last," "only the strong survive," "if you can't stand the heat, get out of the kitchen," and "winning isn't important, it is everything." Associating such expressions with a natural law of biology gives them an aura of respectability, causing the more repugnant consequences of stomping out business competition to be nothing more than carrying out a fundamental law of the universe.

First of all, evolution is a physical phenomenon, like gravity or inertia. How can ruthless rub-outs of business competitors be immoral if it is simply the natural order of things? Second, by implication, evolution means "progress"—the creation of "higher" forms of life at the expense of "lower" forms. So what if the Mom-and-Pop corner grocery store gets crowded out by a giant supermarket? Mom and Pop's grocery was old-fashioned and obsolete and couldn't compete. The new 24-hour supermarket taking up the whole block represents progress through natural evolution of business enterprises and, therefore, is not only justified but desirable.

As a consequence, competition in business circles has become glorified activity. Competition supposedly brings out our best and causes superior performance. Ah, the vitality of it all. To strive, to strain, to bust one's gut to beat out others, to clutch and grasp for success, to attain perfection. That's what it's all about, isn't it? Isn't that why *Winning Through Intimidation* and *Looking Out for Number One* became best-sellers?

By pulling the cloak of natural selection over an idea, one can justify practically any aggressive activity—whether it be munching up business competitors, climbing over co-workers on the corporate ladder, or running up the score in a football game. Darwin must spend lots of time rolling over in his grave these days because, if he were alive, he would object bitterly. Darwin's Darwinism does not assume that evolution means "higher," or that natural means "good," or that selection means "progress."

But philosophical underpinnings are not the issue here. What is really interesting is the basic concept itself. Does evolution in the biological sense actually occur in business? Does a process of natural selection operate through competition to create superior enterprises and more productive institutions? Do things really work that way? Does competition operate in economics as a driving force for the evolution of businesses, and does the degree of such evolution depend upon the intensity of competition?

Most citizens of capitalism would answer with a hearty, "You bet your booties, it does." Things do change in the business world, and, superficially at least, it would seem competition between rivals is the driving force. Business Darwinism seems to be a valid concept. However, before committing to this idea, there is something new to consider. In the field of biology, some of Darwin's ideas are being challenged. As a result, their analogy to business affairs might not be so apt.

There is a prominent body of thought that holds that Darwin had it wrong! Competition exists in nature all right, but evolution occurs when competition is *lacking* rather than when it exists. Based on evidence uncovered by paleontologists and taxonomists, biological evolution does not occur as a gradual, steady process. Instead, it happens in short, sudden bursts, followed by long periods of no change, or stasis. The leading edge of biological thought calls this "Punctuated Equilibrium." What causes these sudden jumps in evolution? The latest theory says it is triggered after a catastrophic disaster causes most competitors to become extinct, such as a comet hitting the earth or a sudden global change in the weather.

After a natural disaster wipes the biological slate clean, unexploited environments appear in the aftermath—niches free of crowded rivals. That is when mother nature's creative ingenuity goes into high gear. New species and novel forms rapidly evolve to fill the newly available environments that, for once, are free of blood-thirsty, tooth-and-fang competition.

Mammals coexisted with dinosaurs for 100 million years but were never a competitive threat. During that time, mammals were nothing more than hairy little rat-like critters scurrying around at night out of the dinosaurs' way. Then, about 65 million years ago, a horrific environmental catastrophe occurred known as the Cretaceous/Tertiary (K/T) mass extinction, which resulted in many species dying out, most notably dinosaurs. It wasn't until the Cretaceous/Tertiary extinction wiped out the dinosaurs that mammalian evolution took off. Bats, whales, horses, rabbits, lions, tigers, and bears—they appeared only after their more established, reptilian competitors had been exterminated. For a period of time, diversification of mammalian species proliferated at an autocatalytic rate.

Interestingly enough, once all of the exposed environmental niches were filled by mammals, evolution once again slowed to a crawl. No new models have come forth in a long time because, after the available niches filled up and the occupants became firmly established, new varieties had little chance for survival. They were quickly squelched by dominant life forms soon after they hatched, so their genes never got a chance to become established. At least that is what the new theory proposes. As neurobiologist W. H. Calvin wrote,

> A niche once occupied will tend to resist new entries. Wedging in via displacing another species is far harder than occupying an empty niche.

Stop and think about it. Doesn't that scenario more closely fit as a business analogy? Isn't it true that dramatic jumps in business enterprises happen *after* some new niche opens up? When the automobile was invented, numerous car manufacturers came into existence. It's fun to peruse the variety of makes once sold in America—La Salle, Maxwell, Pierce-Arrow, Hupmobile, Nash, Cord, Dusenburg, Packard, Studebacker, Hudson—all now long gone. By the 1960s, only three brand names were left of any consequence. Competition had done in the others, and the bloated survivors effectively stifled newcomers. (Did I hear someone just now mention the name Tucker?) Once GM, Ford, and Chrysler cornered the market, stability and stagnation ruled.

Then the catastrophe occurred: oil shortages and economic reversals. Suddenly a new niche appeared—a market for cheap, economical, trouble-free cars. There was no previously existing competition for vehicles featuring those characteristics. That is when new innovations appeared and overseas manufacturing companies sprang onto the American auto scene. The old, established American car manufacturers didn't lose out because of superior competition. They declined because they didn't bother competing in the same market. Japanese automakers gained a big advantage when U.S. companies didn't climb into the ring with them. At the same time, the Japanese studiously avoided competing where competition already existed—the market for large, standard-sized cars.

But, say you, aren't we overlooking a vital factor? Wasn't Detroit's real problem cheap foreign labor? If that's the case, doesn't it get right back to not being able to compete effectively? Where does it say that Detroit has to live with high-priced labor? The idea that modern industries are "sessile organisms" is archaic. Today, industries go where the markets are, whether it be sales or labor. Cheap labor markets are an environmental niche for business just as much as a new sales market. So Volkswagen cars are manufactured in Brazil, and Mercury outboard motors are made in Mexico. No, the basic problem was that Detroit short-sightedly delayed crawling out of its shrinking niche into the new niches opening up next door.

You can point to model after model where this same pattern has occurred. Once nooks and crannies of a business are filled, competition becomes static until a new niche opens up. In my own field, the same cast of giant CPA firms has dominated the nation's audit business for over 60 years. They shuffle a few clients between one another from time to time, but no new upstart ever cracks their cabal. Potential competition from lower-ranking CPA firms is stifled by the King Kong influence of the big firms.

The lesson is, once someone captures an economic mountain, others find it excruciatingly difficult to claw their way to the top. As a result, dramatic changes in business happen most often only after intrusion of catastrophic outside influences, or else by the opening up of a new territory (a new mountain). Economic upheavals from wars, depressions, and political instability are catastrophes. New technologies and new markets provide new mountains to climb. When these things occur, competition once again becomes an effective driving force, but only because there is room for competitors to grow, co-exist, expand, compete, make mistakes, and innovate. That is why the majority of new ideas in business arises when new fields provide wide-open opportunities for entrepreneurs—the punctuated phase of an economic activity. Look at the business spin-offs from space exploration, for example.

However, once equilibrium sets in and the expanding, competitive phase ends, established winners characteristically spend modest amounts on R&D. The field of endeavor becomes controlled by a few dominant firms, and stagnant complacency sets in. Is that, perhaps, why U.S. manufacturers got caught sitting fat, dumb, and happy while foreign companies expanded into new fields of technology, such as silicon-chip applications?

In reality, competition in the traditional capitalistic sense exists only as a transitory phenomenon and only in immature industries. The PC-computer business teemed with competing companies initially. Now it has settled down into the familiar pattern—a few dominant companies (three, to be exact) slicing up the market pie, and the rest starving to death on a few crumbs.

Do you see the implications this has for small business? Heed the lessons of mother nature. Successful operation of a small business is not a matter of picking up a club and jumping into a free-for-all fray. Certainly you can go about it that way and, if you are the quintessent Mutant Ninja small business person, perhaps you should. But chances are best if you seek a competition-free zone rather than to try to out-compete thousands of others in the same ring. In other words, concentrate on finding yourself an empty niche.

Want an empty-niche example? Not long ago, a small company sprang up in Massachusetts that manufactures style-conscious clothing for overweight children. The company produces extra-large sizes for juniors that major clothing manufacturers won't fiddle with because of small volume. Sales are by catalog, so customers won't feel embarrassed walking into a fat person's store. The little company is knocking 'em dead. Why? Because it is a classic empty-niche situation. No one else is doing it and, as long as a famine doesn't occur, there will always be a bountiful supply of fat kids.

Think of it this way: The world of small business consists of a large number of arenas filled with gladiators and lions. Obviously, your chances for survival are better in an arena that contains relatively few gladiators and lions. Or, better yet, none at all. Okay, if that isn't available, how about out-of-shape gladiators and toothless lions? The point is, choose carefully where you are going to fight.

The moral is: Avoid competition until such time competition is no longer avoiding you.

There's an old saying that three things are important in business: location, location, and location. But people tend to be provincial when looking for a location. They are inclined to investigate no farther than the borders of their own hometown. The greatest potential might exist in Phoenix, Arizona. That is where one of my most successful clients moved when his home-town opportunities dried up. He correctly interpreted the above principle to mean: Live where you decide to locate your business rather than locate your business where you decide to live.

EPILOGUE

To as great extent as ever, Americans believe that
"small is beautiful" in our economy. The successful
[presidential] candidate will demonstrate that he shares
this value—after a period in which many voters have
come to believe that the "big guys" get the breaks.
Peter Hart and Geoffrey Garin

I have the good fortune to live on an island. One of its delights is "having" to commute by ferry boat every day to my downtown office in a big city. It's a spiritual interlude—quaffing marine air, feeling the embrace of sea breezes, watching the waves and gulls and boat traffic. (I'm not telling you the location because the ferries are becoming crowded. Heaven forbid more people move here.)

Every morning, we island commuters, several thousand strong, drive to the island ferry terminal and climb aboard. Many immediately head for the concessionaire coffee shop the transportation department so thoughtfully provides. Not with much enthusiasm, however. Being a low-ball, low-bid monopoly operation, the ferry boat coffee shop leaves much to be desired. Coffee and doughnuts are stale, eggs and hashbrowns are slathered in grease, and service and surroundings are insipid.

Predictably, grumbles and gripes of a mere few thousand tax-paying customers have never been enough to motivate civil-service-entrenched transportation department bureaucrats. So the concession has remained an example of what I hear stores in the Soviet Union are like.

THE SECOND COMING OF THE WOOLLY MAMMOTH

A few years ago, though, the inevitable happened. A couple of entrepreneurs happened by sniffing the sweet aroma of opportunity in the air. It was emanating from an empty niche, a niche filled with several thousand affluent commuters enduring poor food and poor service. It was a classic exploitation situation ripe for someone with hustle and imagination and verve. But how could it be taken advantage of when ferry boats are government monopolies?

Easy. If you can't go on board to serve the commuters, serve the commuters before they go on board. The entrepreneurs rented a couple of spaces in the parking lot next to the ferry terminal. There, they set up shop with a small vendor's cart and began to sell good, fresh coffee, fresh pastries, fruit juices, and cereals—all served with a smile and a cheerful greeting.

Grateful commuters flocked around their little establishment, snatching up their wares and carrying the goodies on board where they exchanged sneers with the ferry boat personnel. Naturally, the transportation department tried to put the kibosh on the operation but found its hands were tied because the cart was on private property and was in compliance with town ordinances.

After a time, the entrepreneurs built an even bigger cart covered with a bright awning. Business boomed. Next, noticing their space was close to a utility pole, the entrepreneurs tapped into electrical service and built a tastefully decorated little house on skids complete with heaters, espresso machines, and refrigerators. All of this, mind you, on a commercial parking lot. Their service expanded to espresso products and more breakfast and health food items. For homeward-bound commuters, they began selling prepackaged convenience dinners.

I must tell you it gives me a lift watching this flourishing little enterprise. Although it is small in scale, it brims with vitality and exemplifies everything we've talked about in this book. And it reminds me every day that a remarkable thing has happened. Small business has always enjoyed high esteem in our culture, but primarily out of sentiment rather than from being an economic force. People such as I have always been concerned for the basic survival of small business in the face of crushing competition from big business.

Today, people feel as sentimental as ever toward small business, only now it is looked upon as an economic savior rather than an endangered species. The winds of change have been blowing hard. Many structural transformations have occurred in economics, politics, and society that have been detrimental to big business but favorable to small business.

The environment is different. It is now small business that is running rampant providing jobs and opportunities. To be sure, big business dinosaurs will always be with us and will always be economically important. Technology and economies of scale dictate this be so. But, increasingly, big businesses will come under the umbrella of government protection and subsidies. Otherwise, foreign enterprises will wipe them out. Ironically, it is now big business in America that is worried about survival.

As we adjust to our new service-based economy, some people worry that America's job market will degenerate into nothing more than taking in one another's laundry. I don't pretend to know what the future holds. But I do know I am much more encouraged today than I was twenty years ago. The vitality and resourcefulness of the American entrepreneur is most heartening. When you have had a front-row seat for observing small business as I have had, you come to develop great respect and admiration for the spirit of the American entrepreneur.

Perhaps we will never again see the degree of prosperity and opportunity enjoyed by start-up enterprises during the boom years following World War II, but the ingenuity, enthusiasm, and ambition that drove small business entrepreneurs to affluence in the past are still there. Also spunkiness. A friend of mine on a pre–Tiananmen Square cultural exchange mission asked a leading Chinese intellectual what he thought the main difference was between his country and ours. The Chinese scholar thought for a moment and replied, "Only the brave came to America." With those sorts of things going for us, surely we, the small-business men and women of America, will continue to grow and prosper.

SOURCES

Page 5. Clarence Darrow. *Peter's Quotations*, Dr. Laurence J. Peter (New York: William Morrow & Co., Inc., 1971)

Page 13. For a critique of luck and creativity and their interplay, see Michael LeBoeuf, *Imagineering: How to Profit From Your Creative Powers* (New York: McGraw-Hill, 1980)

Page 17. H. L. Mencken. *A Mencken Chrestomathy* (New York: Alfred A. Knopf, 1949)

Page 27. Jean Shepherd. *In God We Trust: All Others Pay Cash* (New York: Doubleday, 1966)

Page 34. Carl Sandburg. "Wilderness" from *The Complete Poems of Carl Sandburg* (New York: Harcourt Brace Jovanovich, 1970)

Page 38. Ralph Waldo Emerson. *Essays* (New York: Dutton, 1906)

Page 40. *Peter's Quotations* by Dr. Laurence J. Peter (New York: William Morrow & Co., 1971)

Page 41. Maxwell Maltz, M.D. *Psycho-Cybernetics* (Englewood Cliffs, NJ: Prentice-Hall, 1960)

Page 44. Vince Lombardi. *Book of Quotations* (New York: Barnes & Noble, 1987)

Page 51. Seneca. *Peter's Quotations*, Dr. Laurence J. Peter (New York: William Morrow & Co., 1971)

Page 75. A. J. Liebling. *Liebling at Home* (New York: PEI Books, Inc., 1982)

Page 77. Berke Breathed. *Classics of Western Literature—Bloom County 1986–1989* (Boston: Little, Brown & Co., 1990)

Page 88. Daniel Boorstin, quoted in *The Confidence Man in American Literature* by Gary Lindberg (New York: Oxford University Press, 1982)

Page 94. Sam C. Dunham. *The Goldsmith of Nome* (Washington, D.C.: The Neal Publishing Co., 1901)

Page 102. W. C. Fields. *Peter's Quotations* by Dr. Laurence J. Peter (New York: William Morrow & Co., Inc., 1971)

Page 109. Woody Allen. "Confessions of a Burglar" from *The New Yorker*, October 18, 1976

Page 115. Lewis Grizzard. *Chile Dawgs Always Bark at Night* (Boston: G. K. Hall & Co., 1990)

Page 119. Gertrude Stein. *Peter's Quotations* by Dr. Laurence J. Peter (New York: William Morrow & Co., Inc., 1971)

Page 129. Martin Mayer. *The Money Bazaars* (New York: Dutton, 1984)

Page 138. Francis Bacon. *The Great Quotations* by George Seldes (Secaucus, NJ: The Citadel Press, 1960)

Page 146. Jonathan Swift. *Gulliver's Travels* (New York: Airmont Publishing Co., 1963)

Page 181. Rochelle Davis. *Happiness Is a Ratfink* (New York: Kanrom, Inc., 1963)

Page 189. Stephen Leacock. *Peter's Quotations* by Dr. Laurence J. Peter (New York: William Morrow & Co., Inc., 1971)

Page 212. Werner Von Braun. *Peter's Quotations* by Dr. Laurence J. Peter (New York: William Morrow & Co., Inc., 1971)

Page 245. Dialogue from the film *Head Office*, Tri-Star Pictures, 1985

Page 252. Peter D. Hart and Geoffrey Garin. "Winning the White House: The Political Dynamics of 1988" from *The Christian Science Monitor*, August 31, 1987